From the Land of Morning Calm

The Asian American Experience

THE ASIAN AMERICAN EXPERIENCE

From the Land of Morning Calm

THE KOREANS IN AMERICA

Ronald Takaki

PROFESSOR OF ETHNIC STUDIES
THE UNIVERSITY OF CALIFORNIA, BERKELEY

Adapted by Rebecca Stefoff

088498

Chelsea House Publishers

New York ✻ *Philadelphia*

On the cover A Korean family portrait, taken around 1900 in Hawaii.

Chelsea House Publishers

EDITORIAL DIRECTOR   Richard Rennert
EXECUTIVE MANAGING EDITOR   Karyn Gullen Browne
COPY CHIEF   Robin James
PICTURE EDITOR   Adrian G. Allen
ART DIRECTOR   Robert Mitchell
MANUFACTURING DIRECTOR   Gerald Levine

The Asian American Experience

SENIOR EDITOR   Jake Goldberg
SERIES DESIGN   Marjorie Zaum

Staff for *From the Land of Morning Calm*
EDITORIAL ASSISTANT   Kelsey Goss
PICTURE RESEARCHER   Pat Burns

Adapted and reprinted from *Strangers from a Different Shore,*
© 1989 by Ronald Takaki, by arrangement with the author
and Little, Brown and Company, Inc.

First Printing

1   3   5   7   9   8   6   4   2

Library of Congress Cataloging-in-Publication Data
Takaki, Ronald T., 1939–
    From the land of morning calm: Koreans in America
        p. cm.—(The Asian American experience)
    Includes bibliographical references and index.

ISBN 0-7910-2181-5.

        0-7910-2281-1 (pbk.)

    1. Korean Americans—History. I. Title. II. Series: Asian American
    experience (New York, N.Y.)
E184.K6T33 1994   93-43713
973'.04957—dc20   CIP

Contents

Koreatown, Los Angeles, in the 1970s—a time when Korean signs, Korean businesses, and Korean families were becoming a newly visible part of American society.

From a Different Shore

AS A CHILD IN HAWAII, I GREW UP IN A MULTICULTURAL corner of America. My own family had roots in Japan and China.

Grandfather Kasuke Okawa arrived in Hawaii in 1866, and my father, Toshio Takaki, came as a 13-year-old boy in 1918. My stepfather, Koon Keu Young, sailed from China to the islands when he was a teenager.

My neighbors were Japanese, Chinese, Hawaiian, Filipino, Portuguese, and Korean. Behind my house, Alice Liu and her friends played the traditional Chinese game of mah-jongg late into the night, the clicking of the tiles lulling me to sleep.

Next to us the Miuras flew billowing and colorful carp kites on Japanese boy's day. I heard voices with different accents, different languages, and saw children of different colors.

Together we went barefoot to school and played games like baseball and *jan ken po*. We spoke "pidgin English," a melodious language of the streets and community. "Hey, da kind tako ono, you know," we would say, combining English, Japanese, and Hawaiian. "This octopus is delicious." Racially and culturally diverse, we all thought of ourselves as Americans.

But we did not know why families representing such an array of nationalities from different shores were living together and sharing their cultures and a common language. Our teachers and textbooks did not explain the diversity of our community or the sources of our unity.

After graduation from high school, I attended a college in a midwestern town where I found myself invited to "dinners for foreign students" sponsored by local churches and clubs like the Rotary. I politely tried to explain to my kind hosts that I was not a "foreign student." My fellow students and even my professors would ask me how long I had been in America and where I had learned to speak English. "In this country," I would reply. And sometimes I would add: "I was born in America, and my family has been here for three generations."

Asian Americans have been here for over 150 years. They are diverse, coming originally from countries such as China, Japan, Korea, the Philippines, India, Vietnam, Laos, and Cambodia. Many of them live in Chinatowns, the colorful streets filled with sidewalk vegetable stands and crowds of people carrying shopping bags; their communities are also called Little Tokyo, Koreatown, and Little Saigon. Asian Americans work in hot kitchens and bus tables in restaurants with elegant names like Jade Pagoda and Bombay Spice. In garment factories, Chinese and Korean women hunch over whirling sewing machines, their babies sleeping nearby on blankets. In the Silicon Valley of California, rows and rows of Vietnamese and Laotian women serve as the eyes and hands of production assembly lines for computer chip industries. Tough Chinese gang members strut on Grant Avenue in San Francisco and Canal Street in New York's Chinatown. In La Crosse, Wisconsin, Hmong refugees from Laos, now dependent on welfare, sit and stare at the snowdrifts outside their windows. Asian American engineers do complex research in the laboratories of the high-technology industries along

Route 128 in Massachusetts. Asian Americans seem to be everywhere on university campuses.

Today, Asian Americans belong to the fastest growing ethnic group in the United States. Kept out of the United States by immigration restriction laws in the 19th and early 20th centuries, Asians have recently been coming again to America. The 1965 immigration act reopened the gates to immigrants from Asia, allowing 20,000 immigrants from each country to enter every year. In the early 1990s, half of all immigrants entering annually are Asian.

The growth of the Asian American population has been dramatic: In 1960, there were only 877,934 Asians in the United States, representing a mere one half of 1% of the American people. Thirty years later, they numbered about seven million, or 3% of the population. They included 1,645,000 Chinese, 1,400,000 Filipinos, 845,000 Japanese, 815,000 Asian Indians, 800,000 Koreans, 614,000 Vietnamese, 150,000 Laotians, 147,000 Cambodians, and 90,000 Hmong. By the year 2000, Asian Americans will probably represent 4% of the total United States population. In California, Asian Americans already make up 10% of the state's inhabitants, compared with 7.5% for African Americans.

Yet very little is known about Asian Americans and their history. Many existing history books give Asian Americans only passing notice—or overlook them entirely. "When one hears Americans tell of the immigrants who built this nation," Congressman Norman Mineta of California observed, "one is often led to believe that all our forebearers came from Europe. When one hears stories about the pioneers going West to shape the land, the Asian immigrant is rarely mentioned."

Indeed, many history books have equated "American" with "white" or "European" in origin. In his prize-winning study, *The Uprooted*, Harvard historian Oscar Handlin presented—to use the book's subtitle—"the Epic Story of the Great Migrations that Made the American People." But Handlin's "epic story" completely left out the "uprooted" from lands across the Pacific Ocean and the "great migrations" from Asia that also helped to make "the American people." As Americans, we have origins in Europe, the Americas, Africa, and also Asia.

We need to include Asians in the history of America. How and why, we ask in this series, were the experiences of these various groups—Chinese, Japanese, Korean, Filipino, Asian Indian, and Southeast Asian—similar to and different from each other? Comparing the experiences of different nationalities can help us see what events were particular to a group and also highlight the experiences they all shared.

Why did Asian immigrants leave everything they knew and loved to come to a strange world so far away? They were "pushed" by hardships in the homelands and "pulled" by demands for their labor in Canada, Brazil, and especially the United States. But what were their own fierce dreams— from the first enterprising Chinese miners of the 1850s in search of "Gold Mountain" to the recent refugees fleeing frantically on helicopters and leaking boats from the ravages of war in Vietnam?

Besides their points of origin, we need to examine the experiences of Asian Americans in different geographical regions, especially Hawaii compared with the mainland. The time of arrival also shaped their lives and communities. About one million people entered the United States between the California gold rush of 1849 and the 1924 immigration act that cut off the flow of peoples from Asian countries. After a break of some 40 years, a second group numbering about four million came between 1965 and 1990. How do we compare the two waves of Asian immigration?

To answer our questions in these volumes, we must study Asian Americans as men and women with minds, wills, and voices. By "voices" we mean their own words and stories as told in their oral histories, conversations, speeches, and songs as well as their own writings—diaries, letters, newspapers, novels, and poems. We need to know the ordinary people.

So much of history has been the story of kings and elites, as if the "little people" were invisible and voiceless. An Asian American told an interviewer: "I am a second generation Korean American without any achievements in life and I have no education. What is it you want to hear from me? My life is not worth telling to anyone." Similarly, a Chinese immigrant said: "You know, it seems to me there's no use in me telling you all this! I was just a simple worker, a farm worker around here. My story is not going to interest anybody." But others realize they are worthy of attention. "What is it you want to know?" an old Filipino immigrant asked a researcher. "Talk about history. What's that . . . ah, the story of my life . . . and how people lived with each other in my time."

Their stories can enable us to understand Asians as actors in the making of history and as people entitled to dignity. "I hope this survey do a lot of good for Chinese people," a Chinese man told an interviewer from Stanford

University in the 1920s. "Make American people realize that Chinese people are humans. I think very few American people really know anything about Chinese." Elderly Asians want the younger generations to know about their experiences. "Our stories should be listened to by many young people," said a 91-year-old retired Japanese plantation laborer. "It's for their sake. We really had a hard time, you know."

The stories of Asian immigrations belong to our country's history. They need to be recorded in our history books, for they reflect the making of America as a nation of immigrants, as a place where men and women came to find a new beginning. At first, many Asian immigrants—probably most of them—saw themselves as sojourners, or temporary migrants. Like many European immigrants such as the Italians and Greeks, they came to America thinking they would be here only a short time. They had left their wives and children behind in their homelands. Their plan was to work here for a few years and then return home with money. But, after their arrival, many found themselves staying. They became settlers instead of remaining sojourners. Bringing their families to their adopted country, they began putting down new roots in America.

But, coming here from Asia, many of America's immigrants found they were not allowed to feel at home in the United States. Even their grandchildren and great-grandchildren still find they are not viewed and accepted as Americans. "We feel that we're a guest in someone else's house," said third generation Ron Wakabayashi, National Director of the Japanese American Citizens League, "that we can never really relax and put our feet on the table."

Behind Wakabayashi's complaint is the question: Why have Asian Americans been considered outsiders? America's immigrants from Pacific shores found they were forced to remain strangers in the new land. Their experiences here were profoundly different from the experiences of European immigrants. Asian immigrants had qualities they could not change or hide—the shape of their eyes, the color of their hair, the complexion of their skins. They were subjected not only to cultural and ethnic prejudice but also to racism. Unlike the Irish and other groups from Europe, Asian immigrants were not treated as individuals but as members of a group with distinctive physical characteristics. Regardless of their personal merits, they sadly discovered, they could not gain acceptance in the larger society.

Unlike European immigrants, Asians were victimized by laws and policies that discriminated on the basis of race. The Chinese Exclusion Act of 1882 barred the Chinese from coming to America because they were Chinese. The National Origins Act of 1924 totally prohibited Japanese immigration.

The laws determined not only who could come to America but also who could become citizens. Decades before Asian immigration began, the United States had already defined the complexion of its citizens: the Naturalization Law of 1790 had specified that naturalized citizenship was to be reserved for "whites." This law remained in effect until 1952. Unlike white ethnic immigrants from countries like Ireland, Asian immigrants were denied citizenship and also the right to vote.

But America also had an opposing tradition and vision, springing from the reality of racial and cultural "diversity." Ours has been, as Walt Whitman celebrated so lyrically, "a teeming Nation of nations" composed of a "vast, surging, hopeful army of workers," a new society where all should be welcomed, "Chinese, Irish, German,—all, all, without exceptions." In the early 20th century, a Japanese immigrant described in poetry a lesson that had been learned by farm laborers of different nationalities—Japanese, Filipino, Mexican, and Asian Indian:

> *People harvesting*
> *Work together unaware*
> *Of racial problems.*

A Filipino immigrant laborer in California expressed a similar hope and understanding. America was, Macario Bulosan told his brother Carlos, "not a land of one race or one class of men" but "a new world" of respect and unconditional opportunities for all who toiled and suffered from oppression, from "the first Indian that offered peace in Manhattan to the last Filipino pea pickers." Asian immigrants came here, as one of them expressed it, searching for "a door into America" and seeking "to build a new life with untried materials." He asked: "Would it be possible for an immigrant like me to become a part of the American dream?"

This series invites students to learn how Asian Americans belong to the larger story of the rich multicultural mosaic called the United States of America.

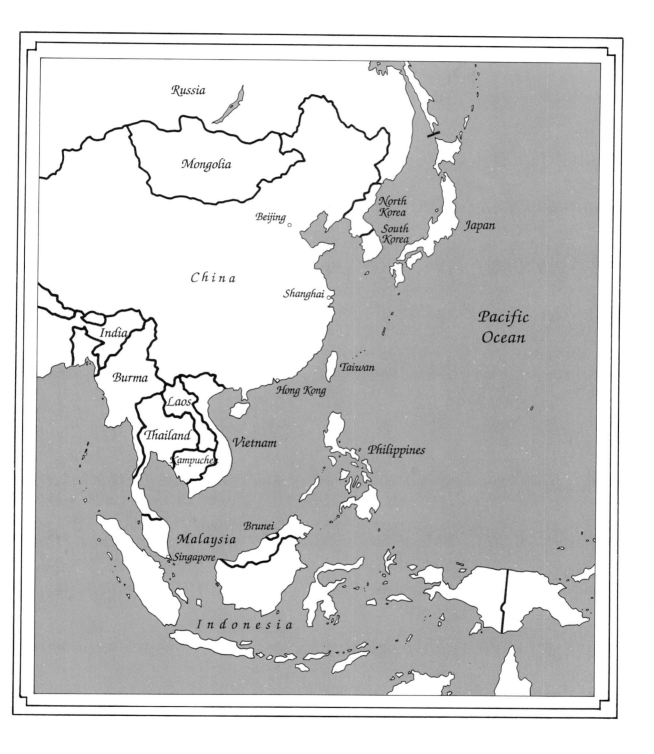

A student at the Korean Boarding School in Honolulu in 1910.
In the early years of the 20th century, most Korean immigrants arrived in
Hawaii rather than on the U.S. mainland.

Chapter One

Leaving the Land of Morning Calm

IN THE EARLY YEARS OF THE 20TH CENTURY, A HIGH-school teacher in Korea took a step that would eventually lead him to America. He joined a secret Korean patriotic society. The teacher's name was Sa-sun Whang. Like many Koreans, Whang wanted to see his homeland freed from the domination of the Japanese, who were colonizing Korea. The Japanese harshly punished any Koreans who spoke out in favor of Korean independence. Said Whang, "At the time, the Japanese military government persecuted the people, especially the young people, and took them to jail."

Before long, Whang was in danger of being arrested by the Japanese police for belonging to the patriotic society. To escape arrest, he fled Korea and went to China. It was a perilous journey. "My wife and I sneaked out. . . . ," he recalled. "We crossed the Yalu River and from there rode the railroad to Shanghai. At that time I wore Chinese clothes. The Japanese didn't know I was Korean; they thought I was Chinese." From China, Whang and his wife were able to move on to their final destination—they boarded a ship bound for the United States. "When I left Korea, I felt like a free man," Whang recalled later. "Korea was like a jail, and I was a prisoner. I wanted to come to America. America was a free country."

Sa-sun Whang and his wife were not alone in leaving Korea. They were part of a wave of immigration that brought about 8,000 Korean men and women to America between 1903 and 1920. Most of them left their homeland—which they called the kingdom of Choson, meaning "Morning Calm"—for Hawaii, which became a U.S. territory in 1900. Approximately 1,000 Koreans went to the U.S. mainland.

The Korean immigrants were young; nearly all of the adults were between 16 and 44 years old. Unlike the earlier Chinese and Japanese immigrants, most of whom came from farming communities, the Koreans came from the cities. They were urban laborers, government clerks, students, policemen, miners, domestic servants, and even Buddhist monks. As a group, they were well educated. About 70% of them could read and write.

Nearly half of the Korean immigrants were Christians. They had been converted by American missionaries, who also encouraged them to go to the United States. A member of the Korean Christian Movement of Hawaii explained how American missionaries appeared in Korea and began telling the Koreans about "the wonderful story of the Cross." After they became Christians, the Koreans were told that Hawaii was a "haven of peace and plenty."

The migration from Korea was also driven by political events. Conflict had been simmering between Japan and Korea since the 1870s. In 1904, Japan invaded Korea. Six years later, Japan formally claimed control of Korea, which remained under Japanese occupation until World War II ended in 1945. Many Koreans went to Hawaii to escape from Japanese domination. "There was little or no opportunity for my grandfather to find a job in Korea in those days," a Korean in Hawaii explained. "The Japanese imperial government was controlling Korea at the time and the outlook toward the future was very poor." The Japanese were "cruel oppressors," he added. "When my grandfather learned that the Japanese government was letting people out of the country to work in the islands, he was happy to volunteer."

Hawaii was a place where Koreans could struggle for their homeland's independence. "When I saw my country fall into the hands of the Japanese aggressors," said one man who left Korea, "I was filled with sorrow, but, unable to do much to help, I applied for the status of an immigrant and came to Hawaii hoping to learn something in order to help my country."

Like Sa-sun Whang and his wife, some Korean migrants left as political refugees, fleeing Japanese persecution. One of these refugees was a woman named Myung-ja Sur. Years later, she explained to her grandson why she had left Korea. "Because the Japanese oppression was so severe for all Koreans, especially Korean patriots, I had to flee to Shanghai," she said. She had been a schoolteacher and had taken part in a Korean nationalist demonstration in 1919, passing out Korean flags and copies of the American Declaration of Independence. "The Japanese went crazy," she recalled. "They beat up people and killed thousands of Koreans while many were arrested and later killed." In Shanghai, Sur was arrested by the Japanese secret police and imprisoned for a month. After she returned to Korea, the Japanese followed her everywhere she went. Realizing that she could not be truly free in Korea, she decided to go to the United States and continue her education.

Not all those who left Korea were political refugees, however. Many were pushed from their homes by poverty. Famine and drought had brought suffering to Korea. One American missionary told of the terrible conditions in Korea in the early 20th century, adding that many Koreans were eager to leave the country: "We have never known such unrest

A farmer in Korea in the 1890s. Although most of the Korean immigrants came from cities, some were farmers; economic hard times and political repression made life difficult in both the towns and the countryside.

among the Koreans due to the excitement of so many going to the Hawaiian Islands to work on sugar plantations, and the dreadful hard times. . . . We can't blame them for wanting to go to America."

In a letter to the governor of Hawaii in 1902, an American official in Korea reported, "The severe famine of the past winter made the matter [of emigrating to Hawaii] seem all the more attractive to the people." The next year, a leader of the sugar industry in Hawaii described the arrival of the first group of Korean immigrants. He pointed out that the famine in Korea meant that there would be a good supply of workers for the plantations of Hawaii: "We have just received about fifty laborers and their families from Korea. As the people there are in a starving condition we hope that we shall be able to get a number of them as they seem to be just what our plantations need."

"Times were hard," a Korean immigrant recalled. "The country had been passing through a period of famine years. . . . My occupation as tax collector barely kept me from starvation's door as I travelled from village to village." At first he planned to migrate alone and return to Korea after three years, but he finally decided to take his family with him to America.

Another Korean explained, "We left Korea because we were too poor." Crying at the memory of the suffering her family had undergone, she added, "We had nothing to eat. There was absolutely no way we could survive." Echoing her story, another migrant said, "There were no opportunities for work of any kind and conditions were bad. It was then that we heard of a man who was talking a lot about the opportunities in Hawaii. He said it was a land of opportunity where everybody was rich."

From newspaper advertisements and posters, Koreans learned that plantation laborers in Hawaii received free housing, medical care, and $16 a month in exchange for working 60 hours each week. These wages were a small fortune to Koreans. People who asked about going to Hawaii were told by the labor recruiters that Hawaii was a "paradise" where "clothing grew on trees, free to be picked," and where "gold dollars were blossoming on every bush." America was described as a "land of gold" and a "land of dreams." Lured by fantasy and hope, Koreans borrowed money from a bank run by the Hawaiian sugar planters. The $100 loan for their passage to Hawaii would be deducted by the plantation managers from their monthly pay over three years.

The Korean migration included women. Of the 6,700 adults who entered Hawaii or the U.S. mainland between 1903 and 1905, nearly 10% were women. Korean men who were going to Hawaii took their wives and children with them because they were guaranteed jobs and housing on the plantations. They saw the islands as a place where family life was possible. But they also took their families with them because they were afraid that they would not be able to return to a Korea that was dominated by the Japanese.

A thousand more Korean women came to America as picture brides between 1906 and 1923. These women married Korean men who were living in Hawaii or on the U.S. mainland. The brides and grooms exchanged photographs and perhaps letters with one another, but they did not meet before they were married. Korean women who wished to become picture brides had to rely on Japanese agents to make the arrangements for them. In their offices in the port cities, agents displayed pictures of men who were seeking wives and took applications from women who were interested in marriage. By 1920, more than one-fifth of all the Korean immigrants in the United States were women.

Most Korean picture brides were young—20 years younger than their husbands, on average. These hopeful young women, arriving on the docks of Hawaii or San Francisco, were sometimes shocked to find that their husbands did not look at all like the pictures they had seen—many men sent photographs that had been taken when they were much younger. Some picture brides, startled and disappointed to discover that the men were so much older than themselves, cried out in dismay or even fainted on the docks.

"*Aigo omani,*" they said, which means: "Oh, dear me, what shall I do?" One of these startled brides was Woo Hong

*From Korean ports like
this one, emigrants
embarked on crowded
steamships for what
they hoped would be a
brighter life.*

Pong Yun. Arriving in the islands at the age of 23, she saw a 36-year-old man greeting her as her new husband. "When I see him," she said years later, "he skinny and black. I no like. No look like picture. But no can go home." Another Korean picture bride, finding that the man she had come to Hawaii to marry did not look like his picture, shut herself in a room and cried for eight days. "But I knew that if I don't get married," she said, "I have to go back to Korea on the next ship. So on the ninth day I came out and married him. But I don't talk to him for three months." A few of the brides indignantly returned to Korea, but most of them, eager to start a new life, decided to remain and make the best of their marriages.

For these young women, America promised a better life than they could expect at home. "My parents were very poor," said a Korean woman. "One year, a heavy rain came, a flood; the crops all washed down. Oh, it was a very hard time. . . . Under the Japanese, no freedom. Not even free talking." She had heard stories about the islands: "Hawaii's a free place,

The first wave of Korean immigration included about 1,500 women. Some were wives; others arrived in America as picture brides, to marry men they had never met.

23

everybody living well. Hawaii had freedom, so if you like talk, you can talk; you like work, you can work. I wanted to come, so, I sent my picture. Ah, marriage! Then I could get to America! That land of freedom with streets paved of gold! Since I became ten, I've been forbidden to step outside our gates, just like the rest of the girls of my days. So becoming a picture bride would be my answer and release."

Picture bride Anna Choi arrived in Honolulu to marry a man she had never met. Her story shows how Hawaii beckoned to women whose horizons were limited in Korea:

> I came to Hawaii as a picture bride not due to the fact that my family was poor but because I had heard so many times about an uncle on my mother's side who was doing quite well for himself in Hawaii. . . . In 1915, I decided to go to Hawaii and asked my mother whether I could be a picture bride, since my uncle's family in Korea knew of a man there looking for a wife. My mother thought I was crazy and tried to persuade me to abandon such a notion, but in vain.

Ties remained strong between political leaders in Korea and the Koreans who lived abroad. This Korean girls' school in Hawaii was founded by Syngman Rhee, who served as president of South Korea from 1948 to 1960.

So, when I was fifteen, equipped with an introduction and a photograph, I boarded a ship at Pusan with five other girls. . . . We boarded another ship at Yokohama after physical examinations, and three long months later we finally arrived at our destination.

When I first saw my fiancé, I could not believe my eyes. His hair was grey and I could not see any resemblance to the picture I had. He was a lot older than I had imagined. . . . He was forty-six years old. . . . I definitely looked on him more as my father than my husband. We were meant to work, I believe, rather than to enjoy our life together.

Hungry for the opportunity and freedom that America offered, many more Korean men and women would have left the Land of Morning Calm if they had been able to do so. But the period during which Koreans were allowed to leave their homeland was short. The Japanese government had two reasons for preventing Koreans from leaving their country: to keep Korean workers from competing with Japanese laborers for jobs in Hawaii, and to cut off the flow of support for Korean independence activities in the United States. In 1905, Japan prohibited Koreans—except for wives and picture brides—from going to the United States.

Because the first wave of immigration from Korea lasted for only a few years, the Korean people came to America in much smaller numbers than the Chinese and Japanese immigrants. Yet, like the other Asian newcomers, the Koreans had high hopes about their lives in the new land. As they crossed the Pacific Ocean to Hawaii, they said to themselves: *"Kaeguk chinch wi"*—"The country is open, go forward."

Koreans in traditional dress. During the passage to Hawaii, many men changed to Western-style suits and cut their long hair—a ritual that symbolized putting aside the old life and preparing for the new.

THE PASSAGE FROM KOREA TO HAWAII WAS A LONG and sometimes frightening trip. One immigrant remembered the uneasy start of the steamship journey: "After boarding, when we got close to the Mokpo River, the turbulence was heavy. We felt the ship rocking and the people in the ship moved like a football and threw up. A voice shouted, 'Every one will die.' I felt we could not live."

As they crossed the sea, Korean immigrants began to prepare themselves for life in the new land. Many of the men put on Western-style suits. At home they had worn their hair long; now they cut it. Aboard one of the ships, a group of Christian Koreans held prayer meetings in the passenger quarters. They became so involved in sharing their faith with their fellow passengers that by the time the ship reached Honolulu they had converted 32 passengers to Christianity and organized a church.

Landing in Honolulu was an exciting moment. When Ch'ang-so Ahn first saw the volcanic mountains of Hawaii rising steeply from the sea before him, he was so moved and overjoyed that he gave himself the pen name *To San* (Island Mountain). But arrival was also a time of great anxiety. Many of the newcomers were so nervous that they could not sleep, wondering what would happen to them in this foreign country. They did not know how to speak English, and they knew nothing about plantation work. They had little time to worry. As soon as they arrived in Honolulu they were rushed to quarantine stations, where they were kept for several days to make sure that they did not have any infectious diseases. Then they were taken to the plantations where they would work and live for the next three years. They settled into their camp quarters—generally large barracks or dormitories for the single men, and private rooms, small houses, or cottages for families. Their new life had begun.

Life on the islands was dominated by sugar. Hawaii's climate was perfect for growing sugar cane on large plantations, and the world's appetite for sugar grew stronger every year. The production of sugar required a lot of labor. Workers were needed to hoe the cane fields, harvest the tall cane stalks, and load the stalks onto wagons or trains to be carried to the mill. At the mill, more workers tended the machinery that crushed the cane and boiled the cane syrup. From the beginning of the sugar industry in Hawaii in the 1830s, the planters faced the constant challenge of finding workers and controlling them.

"Get labor first," the planters said. With enough workers they would make profits, which could be used to buy more land, plant more sugar, and hire more workers. During the second half of the 19th century, the planters made sugar "king" in Hawaii. They were American businessmen and sons of American missionaries who turned the independent island kingdom into an economic colony of the United States.

After 1875, the planters were able to sell sugar to the United States without paying duties, or import taxes. Investments in cane-growing became a "mania," and the production of sugar jumped from 9,400 tons in 1870 to nearly 300,000 tons in 1900. Sugar was Hawaii's most important export.

The growth of the sugar industry depended upon labor for the plantations. The planters, however, did not want to rely on Hawaiian labor. Few native workers were available because the Hawaiian population had been dropping sharply for several decades, largely due to diseases brought to the islands by whites. In addition, Hawaiian workers were not

easily disciplined. They could not be threatened with the loss of their jobs because they could survive by farming and fishing.

So the planters turned to Asia as a source of labor. The first immigrant plantation workers were from China. Later, planters imported laborers from many countries, including Portugal, Japan, Korea, and the Philippines. The planters obtained their workers through companies called labor suppliers; these suppliers recruited workers overseas and arranged for their passage to Hawaii.

When ordering laborers, the planters were careful to build a work force from many different ethnic backgrounds. They did this not because they prized ethnic diversity for its own sake, but because it was easier for them to control a work force that was made up of different nationalities.

The planters used ethnic diversity to break strikes and repress unions. On plantations where the workers were mostly from the same country, laborers cooperated in efforts to raise their pay or improve their working conditions. But on plantations where the workers came from several different coun-

A Korean family in Hilo, Hawaii, around 1915. Families lived in cottages in the plantation camps; single men were less fortunate and had to share large dormitories.

29

*From the Land
of Morning Calm*

*Korean workers and their
families on the Kaeleku Sugar
Plantation on the island of
Maui. Plantation life was hard
and unrewarding. Many
workers left the plantations for
Honolulu and other towns in
Hawaii or on the mainland.*

tries, laborers found it harder to communicate, and in some cases there were ethnic rivalries between them. Members of different groups were less likely to form unions or go on strike together for better pay. One plantation manager advised his fellow planters to employ as many different nationalities as possible to "offset" the power of any one group.

In 1900, Hawaii became a territory of the United States. Laws that had been passed to keep Chinese from immigrating to the U.S. mainland now applied to the islands, and the planters could no longer import Chinese laborers. Worried that the Japanese workers were "getting too numerous," the planters looked for new sources of labor. Their favorite method of dividing the work force was to split it "about equally between two Oriental nationalities," so they turned to Korea. They planned to pit Korean workers against the "excess of Japanese."

Korean workers were introduced to the plantations in 1903. At that time Japan was preparing to extend its rule over

Korea, and the Japanese and Korean people were hostile toward one another. The planters could be pretty sure that the Koreans were "not likely to combine with the Japanese at any attempt at strikes." One planter, angry at his Japanese workers for demanding higher wages, asked a labor company to send him a shipment of Korean workers soon, adding that he thought the planters should employ "a large number of Koreans" and drive the Japanese workers out of the labor market.

The planters took advantage of the rivalry and hostility felt by the two peoples. By pitting Korean against Japanese workers, they hoped to keep both groups from becoming strong enough to challenge the planters. The Japanese workers, who formed the largest ethnic group on the plantations, frequently went on strike against low wages and dismal working and living conditions. When this happened, plantation managers sometimes hired Koreans to do the Japanese workers' jobs and break the strikes. The planters benefited from the division between the two ethnic groups.

But the Korean labor supply ended when Japan banned emigration from Korea to Hawaii in 1905. Once again, the planters had to find a new source of workers to plant and harvest the cane fields and labor in the sugar mills. They turned to the Philippines. By this time, however, nearly 7,000 Korean men, women, and children had become part of Hawaii's plantation world.

It was a world of hard work. Laborers followed a set routine, day after day, working six days every week—seven days during the harvest season. Plantation workers got up at about five o'clock and had half an hour to eat and get ready for the day's work. Then they were taken by trucks or small trains to the fields. The work day began promptly at six.

Laborers were supervised by foremen, called *lunas* in Hawaiian; most of the lunas were white men. Each luna was in charge of about 250 workers, usually 200 men and 50 women. Many women worked because their families needed the money they could earn. The women also did other jobs in the camps, such as cooking and washing clothes.

"The sugar cane fields were endless," a Korean worker said, recalling the long hours she had spent cutting cane stalks twice her height. "Now that I look back, I thank goodness for the height, for if I had seen how far the fields stretched, I probably would have fainted from knowing how much work was ahead. My waistline got slimmer and my back ached constantly from bending over all the time to cut the sugar cane. Sometimes I wished I was a dwarf so that I would not have to bend down constantly."

Another worker complained bitterly about the use of physical punishment to enforce the harsh plantation rules. Korean workers, he said, were "treated no better than cows or horses. . . . Every worker was called by number, never by name. During working hours, nobody was allowed to talk, smoke, or even stretch his back. A foreman kept his eyes on his workers at all times. When he found anyone violating working regulations, he whipped the violator without mercy." An old Korean woman told an interviewer, "I'll never forget the foreman. . . . He said we worked like 'lazy.' He wanted us to work faster. . . . He would gallop around on horseback and crack and snap his whip."

The workday ended at four-thirty in the afternoon. Upon returning to the camp, the workers ate, bathed, and went to bed to rest for the next day's work. Many of the field workers, however, suffered from sunburn so severe that they were unable to sleep.

The men's wages ranged from 65 cents to $1.25 a day; the women earned 55 to 65 cents a day. One immigrant who began work on a plantation in 1903 later calculated that men earned about $16 a month and women $12.50. Out of this income each person had to pay about $6 a month for food and another $1 for laundry service. Many of the workers could barely get by because they also had to send money home to their families in Korea.

One of the first Korean men to immigrate to Hawaii later described the early years on the plantation this way:

> The supervisor or foreman was called luna in Hawaiian language and my luna was German. . . . He treated us like cows and horses. If any one violated his orders, he was punished, usually a slap on the face or flagellating [whipping] without mercy. We couldn't protest against the luna's treatment because we were in fear that we would be fired. . . . We carried our number all the time as an identification card, and we were never called by name, but number. I lived in the camp; it was just like the army barracks; wooden floors and we slept on wooden beds or just on the floor, with one blanket over the body.

Medical care was provided to the workers, but it was of poor quality. The doctors who were available spoke English, not Korean, and it was often difficult or even impossible for a sick person to describe his or her symptoms to the doctor, or to understand the doctor's instructions. One im-

The majority of Korean immigrants were Christians; the church played an important role in their lives on the islands. Methodist missionaries operated this home for women and children.

migrant sadly recalled, "I saw with my eyes some of my good friends die in the plantation camps. In fact, one of them died in my lap with an unknown illness after he got back from the doctor."

In the early years, the plantation owners did not provide recreation or sports for their employees. On Sunday, their day off, some workers simply slept all day. Many, however, went to church. Christianity was an important part of life in the Korean plantation community. Koreans who had become Christians before leaving their homeland set up new churches as soon as they had arrived in Hawaii. In 1905, a missionary reported that seven Korean Christian churches were being built on various plantations. He added that some of the plantation owners gave money toward the building of the churches. The planters also paid for a house and traveling expenses for Hyun Soon, a Korean minister on Kauai. The planters hoped that Soon would improve relations between them and their workers, and they felt that churches would help keep the workers peaceful, orderly, and contented. For the same reason, the plantation owners later provided sports programs and other amusements for the workers.

A missionary who visited Hawaii in 1906 was delighted to find "little congregations" of Koreans everywhere in the islands. "In the evening," he wrote, "the sound of their hymns can be heard in most camps." He estimated that one-third of all the Koreans in Hawaii were Christians. Said one immigrant woman, "Wherever Korean immigrants lived there was always a Christian church." She added that the Korean Christian ministers who traveled on the immigrant ships to Hawaii gave inspiration and hope to their fellow voyagers.

The Korean workers also established schools to teach

their children the Korean language and culture, paying the schoolmasters out of their wages. Although they lived in Hawaii, they were determined to raise their children as Koreans. After Japan invaded and took control of Korea, the Koreans in Hawaii felt an even greater need to keep their national spirit alive. Explained one immigrant, "Every Korean overseas thought that Japan would destroy the Korean history and culture, so that we Koreans in America thought we should preserve our culture and urged Koreans to support the Korean school financially." Like the Korean churches, the Korean schools in Hawaii reflected their patriotism and cultural pride.

The Koreans in Hawaii also organized their own governing councils to maintain order among themselves. Each plantation community was governed by a committee called a *dong-hoe,* modeled on the traditional village council of Korea. On a larger scale, the immigrants set up patriotic and nationalist societies to support the anti-Japanese resistance in the homeland. These associations collected dues from members to pay for Korean newspapers, textbooks for the Korean schools, and aid to the independence movement in Korea.

Disgusted with the backbreaking work and low wages, many of the Korean immigrants left the plantations as soon as they could. Many of them went to Honolulu and other Hawaiian towns, where they opened laundries, restaurants, and other businesses. They became part of the multicultural fabric of Hawaiian society. Other Koreans, however, were disappointed that Hawaii had failed to live up to their golden dreams. A thousand of them returned to Korea. But some of them migrated to the U.S. mainland, hoping that it would offer them greater opportunities than they had found in the islands.

A Korean family in 1920s California. Unlike Chinese and Japanese immigrants, who had arrived in America in much larger numbers, the first wave of Koreans did not settle in distinct ethnic communities. They spread among the general population, although, because of racial prejudice, they often had trouble finding places to live.

KOREAN IMMIGRANTS WHO HAD FOUND HARDSHIP
and disappointment in the plantation world of Hawaii crossed
the sea once again, looking for jobs, homes, and security on
the U.S. mainland. "Opportunities in the Hawaiian Islands
were very limited," recalled Meung-son Paik. "We heard of
unlimited opportunities on the mainland." Paik's father borrowed money for steamship fare and took his family to San
Francisco in 1906.

By 1907, a thousand Koreans had come to the mainland. Nearly all of them settled in the West. Many went
inland, working in the copper mines of Utah, in the coal mines
of Colorado and Wyoming, and on the railroads in Arizona.
A few went north to Alaska's salmon fisheries. Most settled
in California. In 1910, two-thirds of the Koreans on the U.S.
mainland were living in California. San Francisco and Los
Angeles were centers of Korean cultural and political activity.
Koreans also settled in Dinuba and Reedley, two towns in the
San Joaquin Valley, the heart of California's agricultural
empire. But the number of Koreans on the mainland remained
small: only 1,680 in 1920 and 1,700 in 1940.

Unlike the Japanese and Chinese immigrants, the
Koreans who came to the mainland did not have their own
separate ethnic economy and community. There were not
enough of them to develop Koreatowns in American cities,
with their own stores, merchants, restaurants, services,
churches, schools, and banks. But the Koreans felt a strong
sense of ethnic identity, stronger even than that of the Japanese and Chinese immigrants. The Koreans in America were
united and strengthened by their struggle against the Japanese
occupation of their homeland.

Chapter Three

To the Mainland

Because the Koreans deeply resented the Japanese invasion of Korea, they found it especially infuriating to be confused with the Japanese. Yet many whites simply lumped all Asians together as Japanese. In 1924, a Korean woman said, "No matter where I appeared—whether the library, on the street car, or downtown, I perceived that their [the whites'] attention was fixed upon me and soon there followed a faint but audible whisper, 'Oh, she is a Jap!'" When a Korean newcomer went to a barbershop in Los Angeles, he was told they did not want the "Japanese trade."

In her novel *Clay Walls,* Ronyoung Kim captures the shocked surprise of an immigrant woman who arrived in Los Angeles during this time, only to discover that Americans knew nothing about Korea or Koreans: "Her country's history went back thousands of years but no one in American seemed to care. To her dismay, few Americans knew where Korea was. This was 1920. The United States was supposed to be a modern country. Yet to Americans, Koreans were 'oriental,' the same as Chinese, Japanese, or Filipino."

The schools were not free of racial prejudice and ignorance. One Korean immigrant complained, "During the first days of school life, children would call me 'Jap.' I would protest and sometimes resort to fists, but the most effective means would be total indifference." Another student was annoyed by her high-school history teacher's rude remarks about "Japs." One day she got up in class. "How do you know I'm . . . a Jap?" she asked, insisting she was not Japanese. The teacher then asked, "Who are you then?" Sarcastically she replied, "Are you so ignorant you don't know what a Korean is? And you a history teacher?"

Like other Asians, Korean immigrants were seen as "strangers from a different shore." They experienced much racial discrimination. When they tried to rent houses, they were often refused by white landlords. "In renting a place," a Korean woman recalled, "only the 'junk house' was available. None in the nicer areas in the 'white town.'" Koreans were also refused service in public parks, theaters, and restaurants. In Los Angeles, a Korean man went to a restaurant for lunch. "Although there were not many customers," he said later, "the waitress did not come to my table. After awhile, a young receptionist came to me and said with a low voice that 'we can't serve you lunch, because if we start serving lunch to the Orientals, white Americans will not come here.'"

Koreans also suffered from competition and conflict between Asian and white workers. Like Chinese and Japanese laborers, the Koreans became targets of white workers who feared that Asian immigrants would take their jobs. In 1910, Koreans who had been hired to pick oranges were camped on a farm owned by a California woman. One night, the silence was broken by an attack from white workers. The whites hurled rocks and shouted at the Koreans to leave at once or be killed. The farm's owner stood up for her employees, angrily declaring, "The minority Korean people in this great country of America have a right to live and work just as the other nationalities. They are hard working, diligent and honest people who are struggling for a decent life."

Koreans were also discriminated against by the government. Groups such as the Asiatic Exclusion League were formed to pressure the government to keep Asian immigrants from entering the United States. A law had been passed in

1882 to keep out immigrant laborers from China, and white business and political leaders wanted that law to exclude Japanese and Korean immigrants as well. The flow of Koreans out of their homeland was stopped in 1905 by the Japanese government, but by that time many Koreans who had already gone to Hawaii were migrating again, this time to the mainland. In 1907, President Theodore Roosevelt gave in to anti-Asian pressure and banned the movement of both Japanese and Korean laborers from Hawaii to the mainland. In 1924, all immigration from Asia was banned by a new federal immigration law.

The government also placed obstacles in the path of Koreans who had already come to the mainland. In 1913, California passed a state law called the Alien Land Act, which said that only U.S. citizens and white immigrants could own land. Under this law, Koreans could not become landowners, for they could not become citizens—a federal law dating from 1790 said that only *white* immigrants could become naturalized citizens of the United States. A Korean immigrant remembered how the land law had driven his family out of California: "We left California because the state had passed the alien land act. You couldn't control your farm. Then we went to Washington. But after we lived there for a few years, Washington passed an anti-alien exclusion farm law, so we went to Utah where they did not have such a law." Another Korean recalled the difficulty of owning or even renting land: "If we wanted to rent land, it had to be in a child's name that was born in this country—a citizen. It was impossible as a foreigner."

Although Korean children born in the United States were automatically U.S. citizens, their immigrant parents

could not share the benefits of citizenship. In 1921, an immigrant named Easurk Emsen Charr challenged this ban in the courts. Charr had been drafted into the U.S. Army in 1918. Three years later he went to a federal district court to request citizenship, arguing that his military service should entitle him to become a naturalized citizen. But the court declared that Koreans were "of the Mongol family" and therefore were excluded from becoming citizens. In other words, Charr could not become a citizen because he was not white. The fact that he had served in the U.S. armed forces did not matter.

The Korean community on the American mainland was made up mostly of men. A thousand Koreans came to the mainland from Hawaii between 1905 and 1910. Only 45 of them were women; another 29 were children. A hundred or so Korean picture brides came after 1910, but men still greatly outnumbered women. In 1920, three-fourths of all Koreans on the mainland were men. "Most of the Korean men were

A Korean American family displays its dual heritage: The flags of the United States and Korea flank the front door of their house.

41

alone in those days," an immigrant explained. "They left their families in Korea, so they were bachelors and single men." Many of these "bachelors" were really married men with wives in Korea. For example, of the 74 Korean men who worked for a railroad company, 2 were widowed, 30 were single, and 42 were married but had left their wives in Korea. The lonely Korean men sang love songs from the old country:

Some loves are soft, others are rough.
Some loves are deep like Kuwol Mountain.
Other loves are so sad like the girl who sent her love to
    the army.
Some loves are secret.
What a delight! What a pleasure!
You can't help falling in love.

But there were few Korean women in America to hear them sing.

American cities offered limited job opportunities for Koreans. They could become restaurant workers, gardeners, janitors, and domestic workers. After his arrival in the United States, Sa-sun Whang, the teacher who had fled Korea with his wife to escape political persecution, worked as a house servant. Encountering racism, he discovered that America was not the land of freedom he had imagined. "I felt the discrimination and realized that America was not a free country," he said. "Everybody did not enjoy liberty. The American people saw the Asian people as a different race. They didn't respect the Asian people. I wanted some postal or factory work, but they didn't give it to me. I couldn't get a job."

Outside the cities, Koreans were able to find work as railroad laborers. Sometimes they worked in gangs together with Japanese laborers, but most of the time they formed their own work gangs. "After talking with the foreman of a railroad company," one Korean immigrant recalled, "I entered into a contract with him to provide a 'gang' of Korean workers. The conditions were that we worked repairing railroad tracks, ate and slept in wagons." Railroad laborers were moved from one place to another as work became available in different parts of the West. They had no chance to form stable communities or put down roots.

Most Koreans in America, however, were farm laborers. Using a traditional Korean arrangement, they organized themselves into work teams, usually ten men under the leadership of a supervisor. Their ethnic identity as Koreans guided and motivated these workers, who believed that if they did well, they would help to improve job opportunities for all Koreans. They told one another, "Our only capital today in this land is nothing but honesty; therefore, work diligently without wasting time whether your employer watches you or not; then you will be working not only today but tomorrow and even the whole year round. If your employer has confidence in you, then your friends, Kim, Lee, or Park will also get jobs, because of your hard and honest work. In this way, eventually all Koreans will get jobs anywhere and at any time." These early Korean immigrants believed that they could achieve economic success by sticking together and helping one another—a belief that is still shared by the most recent immigrants from Korea.

The teams of Korean farm workers moved from field to field and from town to town, wherever they could find work. The story of one Korean immigrant shows the constant movement of this working life. Ten days after arriving in San

Francisco in 1916, he went to Stockton. There he joined a team headed by a Korean labor contractor and worked on a bean farm. "There were about 20 other Koreans working there," he said. "We were hoeing the bean fields and when we finished we went to another bean farm for hoeing. It was hard work. . . . Then we went to Dinuba picking grapes. I was flocking with other Koreans, and I went where they went for available farm jobs." The *New Korea*, a newspaper published in San Francisco, described this ebb and flow of farm laborers: "There are not many Koreans in Dinuba, but when it is grape picking time, many Koreans will come. . . . Sacramento is a stopping place for Koreans who go back and forth to work on farms."

The farm workers' day began early in the morning. Waking up at five o'clock, they ate breakfast and then gathered at a meeting place where the farmers assigned jobs. "They told you where to go and who to work with in the fields," a Korean worker recalled. There were orchards of peaches, plums, and grapes, and the workers followed the group leaders to the orchard that was ready to be harvested. There "the men did the picking if the trees were too tall for the women," and the "women, boys, and girls waited on the ground to pack the fruit."

Picking fruit could be dangerous work. Said one laborer, "If you picked grapes you had to be careful where you put your hand in the vines because black widow spiders and yellow-jacket hornets were all over the grapevines." Workers were often bitten and stung. They learned to make mud packs and place them on the wounds to control the swelling. Picking peaches was a slow and tiresome task. The workers had to dust each peach with a feather brush to knock the bugs off the peach fuzz. They also had to check each piece of fruit for marks or holes before packing it in the proper box according to its size.

As the sun rose, the California fields grew hot and dry. "The day starts out around seventy to eighty degrees," said a laborer, "and by noon time the temperature reaches around a . . . hundred and ten degrees." Usually there was "no breeze whatsoever." After working all morning in the blazing sun, the workers looked for a shady spot where they could eat their lunch: "Most of us took our lunch which consisted of rice, kimchi [spicy pickled vegetables], and maybe some beef or chicken. Each of us picked our own tree and ate under the shade and after we finished we usually took a short nap." They started working again at one o'clock and continued until five.

At the end of the workday, said one man, "your arms and legs felt very heavy and your back really ached." When the workers reached their quarters around six o'clock, he added, "everybody fought to take a bath because if you worked

A class photo taken in Dinuba, California, includes Korean children. A number of Korean farm workers settled in Dinuba, located in California's San Joaquin Valley; worshipers from elsewhere in the valley flocked to Dinuba's Korean church.

in the fields your whole body got covered with dirt from head to toe, especially if you picked grapes. When you packed peaches, the fuzz made you itchy."

Work in the tomato fields was equally hard and tiring. Sa-yong Whang was assigned to plant tomato seeds on a farm in Stockton. "Three men worked as a team; the first man dug the hole, the second planted tomato seeds, and the third covered the hole and watered it," he said. As a member of a team, Whang had to keep up with his fellow workers. "Everybody was working faster than I was, and I had a hard time following the other two. I waited for lunch time to come so that I could rest for awhile." But when lunch time came, Whang could not eat his lunch because the weather was so hot and he was so tired. "I laid down on the ground and rested until the others finished their lunch. When I finished my day's work, I hardly could walk back to my rooming house. . . . During the night I was unable to sleep, because my whole body was sore and I felt pains all over."

Over time, some Koreans were able to become independent farmers. Often several of them combined their savings to rent land to farm. "During the years that my father was working as a farm laborer," a Korean said, "he made up his mind that he had to own his own business in order to make money. So, he and a group of friends got together and formed a company and pooled their money together. They were making great profits in potato farming in Stockton."

Many of the Korean enterprises were very successful. In 1918, Korean rice farmers in the Sacramento Valley produced 214,000 bushels of rice. One farmer, Chong-nim Kim, was so productive that he was known as the "rice king" in the

Korean community. By the 1920s, Korean farmers in Willows, California, were cultivating 43,000 acres of rice, and Korean farmers in the San Joaquin Valley were shipping fruit to Korean wholesale markets in Los Angeles.

One of the most successful Korean farmers and businessmen was Hyung-soon Kim. He came to California in 1913, and eight years later he formed a business partnership with Ho Kim. Their business, the Kim Brothers Company, grew into a large operation with its own orchards, nurseries, and fruit-packing sheds. Hyung-soon Kim and an employee named Anderson developed new varieties of peaches, including a "fuzzless peach." The nectarine, a fruit that was created by crossing peaches and plums, also boosted the fortunes of the Kim Brothers Company. "We felt," said Hyung-soon Kim, "that we were the first Orientals who invented a new fruit for the American people and would be the first Korean millionaires in the Korean community."

Korean business activities went beyond agriculture. Koreans also entered the hotel business. The first Korean hotel in Sacramento opened in 1906. By 1920, there were more than 20 Korean-owned hotels in the states of California and Washington. Many Korean hotel owners were labor contractors, who used their hotels to provide room and board for Korean workers and arranged jobs for them. Koreans also opened restaurants and stores, including groceries, tobacco shops, bakeries, and photo studios. But the two most popular businesses were barbershops and laundries. These demanded hard work but could be started with relatively small amounts of money. All of these business enterprises had one thing in common: they let the Koreans work for themselves. Like other

Like other Asian immigrants, Koreans learned that one way to escape racial discrimination in the workplace was to open their own businesses, such as restaurants and barber shops.

Asian immigrants, Koreans turned to self-employment to escape the racial discrimination they faced in the mainstream economy.

Many Korean immigrants believed that their best hope of succeeding in America and overcoming racial discrimination was to become as American as possible. They thought that the Chinese and Japanese immigrants, who had come to the United States before them, had turned white

Americans against them by clinging to their old customs and keeping to themselves.

"The reason why many Americans love Koreans and help us, while they hate Japanese more than ever," a Korean newspaper published in America announced, "is that we Koreans gave up old baseness, thought and behavior, and became more westernized." Korean immigrants tried to learn English. Their leaders told them that to be "accepted and invited again and again to work by the whites," they needed to show that Koreans were trusty, hardworking, and worthy. Koreans also emphasized the fact that, unlike most Chinese and Japanese immigrants, they were Christians, sharing the faith of white America.

A Korean newspaper summed up the achievements of the first Koreans in America: "We came to this country with empty hands, but now we have made some money which enables us to build a new Korean society and send young Koreans to school. Thus, we are very grateful to (the owner of this land) America."

Members of a patriotic organization called Independence to Korea Through Self-Cultivation. Many Koreans in the United States devoted themselves to the cause of Korean nationalism.

ALTHOUGH THEY SPOKE OF BUILDING "A NEW KOREAN society" in America, many Korean immigrants in the United States would not let themselves become permanent settlers. They remained deeply tied to Korea, their homeland. At the heart of their community was the struggle for Korean independence from Japan. They had left the Land of Morning Calm as sojourners, temporary travelers who planned to return to Korea. But when Japan took control of Korea, the immigrants were suddenly cut off from the possibility of going home. They became *yumin*, "drifting people."

The first generation of Koreans in America carried a special burden of suffering, for they had been brutally cut off from their country. Shortly after Japan annexed Korea, a Korean newspaper in America said, "Korea is dead and no person is as sad as the person without a country." Years later, Lee-wook Chang, a well-known Korean educator and community leader, described the feelings of these "people without a country":

> I wonder how many Koreans today will remember the early immigrants who laid the foundation of the Korean community? The life of all early Korean immigrants—pioneers of the Korean community—had been the same everywhere; of loneliness, hardship, and fatigue. The first generation suffered more mentally and physically than the succeeding generations, because Korea was annexed by Japan; they became men without a country. Nobody cared for and looked after them. Nevertheless, more than two thousand Koreans, including the political refugees, did not lose their hope, and thought that their first duty was to work

for the cause of the restoration of national independence from the Japanese domination.

The Korean National Association, a group that was organized in the United States to support the struggle for Korean independence, angrily called for an end to all contact between Japanese and Korean immigrants, saying that "normally one does not associate with the murderer of one's parents, and Japan had murdered our fatherland." Grieving over their loss, the Korean immigrants became even more tightly bound to their homeland. They felt driven by the need to free Korea from Japanese colonialism.

For most Korean immigrants, life in America was organized around the independence movement. As Korean businessmen increased their profits, they gave more money to the patriotic cause. In 1918, for example, Korean rice farmers in the Sacramento Valley contributed $43,000 to the Korean National Association. Many individuals gave more than $1,000. Hyung-soon Kim was typical of the many Koreans who felt close ties to their homeland even after many years in America. He had left Korea to seek freedom from Japanese rule, but he insistently maintained his Korean national identity. In 1975, at the age of 89, he explained that he had fought for Korean independence and wanted to die as a Korean. Asked about his last wish, he replied: "I would like to go back to Korea and work for the country."

Patriotism filled the lives of many immigrants with a strong sense of purpose, community, and identity. "I was earning money then," a Korean woman later recalled, "and decided that I wanted to become a member of the Korean National Association, pay dues to support the Korean newspaper, and also to contribute to the patriotic fund. I gave one-tenth of my pay—which was optional for women, but I felt so good to be able to do so." Taking part in Korea's struggle gave meaning to her life in an America that often seemed bleak and harsh. She said, "On work days, I put on my work clothes and worked in the fields with the men—a lunch bucket hung over my shoulder. Sundays, I would dress up in my clean Sunday clothes and go to worship. I felt no sadness, just lots of enthusiasm and happiness in just being able to do something."

Church was especially meaningful to this woman and many of her fellow Koreans. The immigrants felt that they were a stranded people, and their Christian faith gave them support. As a Korean community leader said, "A people without a country must have something to believe in and to hold on to. In Christian principles we have found a pattern for our future—both as individuals and as a nation." The Korean Methodist Church of San Francisco held its first service in 1905, and the Korean Presbyterian Church was established in Los Angeles a year later. Within 10 years, there were a dozen Korean churches in California. The churches were the religious arm of the patriotic political organizations. Ministers of the churches were also officials of the Korean National Association.

The churches were also social centers for the rural Koreans, who were spread out across the countryside. For example, in Dinuba, California, Koreans from the San Joaquin Valley gathered at church on Sundays to worship, socialize, and renew their commitment to the liberation of their home-land. At church they took part in debates on topics such as "Jesus Christ and the Future of Korea," "The Relationship of

Korea and Christianity," and "The Duty of Koreans Abroad."
One immigrant observed, "If the Koreans gathered together,
it was usually to worship in church or to protest against the
Japanese oppression in Korea." Louise Yim, a Korean patriot
who lived in Los Angeles in the 1920s, agreed. She said, "The
Korean's social life in the United States consisted of two main
activities: politics and religion."

The immigrants felt that education could help them
free Korea from the Japanese. "We can crush the enemy
(Japan) with learning," argued a Korean newspaper, "and
without learning our land is not ours. . . . We can study a full
week, through only 4-5 hours of labor, and only three summer
months of work will finance a year of education. If we are
unable to attend day school, we can always go to night
school." The Koreans passionately pursued learning. By 1920,
Koreans had a higher percentage of adults who could read and
write than any other Asian immigrant group.

Although Korean immigrants worked hard to learn
English to improve their standing in American society, they
did not abandon their native language. They felt that the
Korean language was a vital part of their cultural and national
identity, so in cities and towns throughout California they
established Korean language schools where their American-
born children could study Korean. "Let us think of the future
Korean community of ten years from now," urged a Korean
writer. "If we want to start afresh our Korean community, we
should give serious thought to our children's education and
have schools that would give them a Korean education." The
second generation of Koreans went to Korean language
schools in addition to American schools. "The happiest moment for my parents," said a student, "was when I came home

with the certificate of graduation from my Korean language school."

Family life was organized around Korean nationalism. Mothers were determined to raise their children as Koreans. Children "spoke Korean at home and, when they were old enough, dated Koreans their own age," recalled American-born Gloria Hahn. Young people were sent to Korean churches and taken to Korean independence meetings; they also celebrated the Korean king's birthday. Home, family, church, and nation were one in the Korean community. "My mother stayed home to raise a family," Hahn said, "breaking the monotony of homemaking by being a charter member of the Korean Women's Patriotic League, writing for Korean newspapers, and working actively in her church."

As early as 1903, Korean immigrants in Hawaii organized the New People's Association. Two years later, Koreans in San Francisco organized a similar group. These

Unlike most of the Chinese and Japanese immigrants, the Koreans shared the Christian faith that was common to many of their white neighbors in America. Nonetheless, they suffered the same racial discrimination as other Asian groups.

55

associations helped new immigrants find housing and jobs, but they also led the resistance against Japanese colonialism through speeches, newspaper articles, and fund-raising. Other Korean political organizations soon sprouted in Hawaii and on the mainland. In 1909, these various groups were combined into the Tae-Hanin Kungmin-hoe (THK), the Korean National Association of North America. The THK had headquarters in San Francisco and branches on the mainland and in Hawaii. All Korean immigrants were required to join the THK and pay dues.

Korean patriots in America had different ideas about how Korea's independence could be restored. One group wanted an active, military approach, for example, while another group called for education and diplomacy. Each of these factions within the patriotic movement published its own newspapers and magazines to tell Korean immigrants about nationalist activities in America and in Korea. These publications kept alive the spirit of patriotism and the dream of Korean independence.

A newspaper published by those who favored armed resistance against the Japanese declared, "We shall overcome this crisis by resorting to arms and blood. In order to kill all traitors and to crush the Japanese, it is necessary to resort to pistols and sword and it can be accomplished only through spilling our blood and sacrificing our lives." Training programs were established in the United States to prepare for armed struggle against the Japanese in Korea. In Hawaii, a Korean leader named Yong-man Park formed a military corps of 300 soldiers, and "military academies" were established in Claremont and Lompoc, California. A center for training Korean pilots began operating in Willows, California, in

1920. Six Korean teachers and an American engineer trained 19 student pilots in three airplanes that were donated by Chong-nim Kim, the "rice king." One Korean community leader announced, "When Korea is armed to such an extent that she can meet the foe on something like an even footing, victory will be ours. We Koreans want to be in the fight. Actually, all Koreans have a date with the Japs, and the sooner we are able to keep it, the better."

An observer noted the hatred felt by the Koreans toward the Japanese during the 1930s: "Singly and collectively they hate the Japanese; all Japanese." Anti-Japanese feelings were everywhere in the Korean immigrant community. After the San Francisco earthquake destroyed the build-

In the early 1930s, Michael Kim of Hawaii copied the Bible by hand in his native Korean, producing a monument to Korean Christianity that was likened to the illuminated manuscripts produced by European Christian monks during the Middle Ages.

ings of the Korean Mutual Assistance Association and the
Korean church, the association announced that it did not want
any help from the Japanese. The announcement said, "We are
calling your attention to the fact that we are anti-Japanese, so
we shall not accept any relief fund from the Japanese consu-
late. We shall reject interference of Japanese authorities in our
community affairs in any manner. No matter how great a
plight we are in, we must always refuse Japanese help. We'd
rather die free than under Japanese jurisdiction."

Koreans again scorned Japanese aid after 11 Korean
farm workers were beaten by whites. When a Japanese official
from Los Angeles visited the victims and offered help, the
THK at once protested that a Japanese government official
had no business interfering in Korean immigrant affairs. In a
telegram sent to United States Secretary of State William
Jennings Bryan, the THK explained: "Please regard us not as
Japanese in the time of peace and war. We Koreans came to
America before Japan's annexation of Korea and we will never
submit to her so long as the sun remains in heaven."

Korean hatred for Japan grew as the Koreans realized
how completely they had been cut off from the land of their
birth. "My mother longed to go back to Korea," a daughter
said, "but the thought of the Japanese made her shudder."
Under Japanese rule, Korea had become a "tiger's cage" and
a "snake-hell." Korean immigrants who had returned to their
homeland were shocked by Japanese oppression. They warned
their countrymen in America to stay away from Korea. "It is
very difficult to describe the situation at home," wrote one
immigrant who had returned to Korea, "and it is awfully hard
to live under these conditions. I am chained now, after having

lived freely in America. . . . I have only one request of you—please arrange my passage to America."

Koreans in the United States could not go home again—not until Korea had been freed from Japanese imperialism. "Without National Independence," said an editorial in a Korean American newspaper, "We Have No Country To Return To. We are a conquered people. Occasionally, Koreans in America think they can return home, but they are not thinking whether they have their country or home. How we Koreans in America dare to forget prison-like Korea! and try to return to that place! We must struggle in exile. Yes, we shall return when we have a freedom bell and a national flag."

Grieving over the loss of his homeland, one immigrant urged his fellow immigrants to cling to their Korean identity. They did not want to become "new world citizens," he reminded them. "Now our business should be for all Koreans and our activity should be based on the welfare of our mother country. Thus we are not sojourners, but political wanderers, and we are not laborers but righteous army soldiers." Korean nationalists thought of the THK as a kind of government that could represent them in their dealings with the United States government. A people without a country, they tried to create a new Korea in America.

But they also felt a special mission to liberate their homeland. Safe in the United States, they admired the patriots who were fighting the Japanese in Korea, and they honored the heroes who rose up in armed resistance. They would not let themselves forget the thousands of Koreans who had been wounded and killed struggling against Japanese imperialism. They kept alive stories of Japanese cruelty. Said an immigrant,

A Korean club presents a program of traditional arts in 1927. Through clubs, schools, and churches, immigrants familiarized their children with the language, clothing, and customs of Korea.

"One lady said that her brother had died in Korea from back injuries suffered from persistent Japanese floggings. Another told of the burning of a Christian church filled with a worshipping congregation. A third told of Japanese wholesale mistreatment of Korean-Christians who were tied by the thumbs to the ceiling and left to die by painful hanging." The

anger that these stories aroused in the Koreans in America fueled their determined independence movement.

Korean rage against Japan exploded in 1908 in the assassination of Durham Stevens. Stevens was an American who had been hired by the Japanese government to give Americans a favorable view of the Japanese occupation of Korea. He tried to convince the United States government that the Korean people themselves welcomed and benefited from Japanese rule. To the outraged Korean immigrants, Stevens was a traitor, a "Japanese dog." On his way from Korea to Washington, Stevens stopped in San Francisco, where a local newspaper published his views about Japanese rule in Korea. The Korean community was infuriated. A group of angry Koreans confronted Stevens on a downtown street, and one of them, In-hwan Chang, shot Stevens. Stevens died in the hospital. Chang was charged with murder and sent to prison.

Chang immediately became a national hero for many Korean immigrants. Contributions for his defense flowed generously from Koreans in Korea, Japan, Siberia, China, Mexico, and the United States. Koreans in America gave the most; many of them donated an entire week's earnings. In court, Chang made the following statement: "I was born on March 30, 1875, in a northern Korean province and became a baptized Christian in my early age. When I saw my country fall into the hands of the Japanese, I was filled with sorrow, but I was unable to do much to help. I came to Hawaii as an immigrant to learn something in order to help my country. . . . While hundreds of thousands of Koreans are dying at the hands of the Japanese invaders, Stevens has the effrontery to invent the lie that the Koreans are welcoming their Japanese aggressors. . . . To die for having shot a traitor is a glory, because I did it for my people."

A Korean newspaper in San Francisco praised the assassination of Stevens, saying, "Come Patriots! Come Patriots! Let us wake by the sound of the pistol. . . . It is right to attack everyone who hurts our compatriots and our country, so that every one of our 20,000,000 people may fight for the liberty and independence of our country to the end." One Korean woman commented that at this time the Korean immigrants were "insane about independence."

Patriotic fury was the driving emotion of many Koreans in the United States. As immigrant Younghill Kang sadly observed in his 1937 novel *East Goes West,* these single-minded patriots lived "in a narrow world." They were interested only in events in Korea, ignoring everything else in the world around them. Kang saw that many of the Koreans in America were bound to their past by the loss of their country, unable to have a future in the United States. He wrote, "With Korean culture at a dying gasp, being throttled wherever possible by the Japanese, with conditions at home ever tragic and uncertain, life for us was tied by a slenderer thread to the homeland than for the Chinese. Still it was tied. Koreans thought of themselves as exiles, not as immigrants." Pak, a character in *East Goes West,* lives in this narrow world of Korean nationalism:

> [Pak] was a most typical Korean, an exile only in body, not in soul. Western civilization had rolled over him as water over a rock. He was a very strong nationalist; so he always sat in at the Korean Christian services,

because they had sometimes to do with nationalism. With his hard-earned money, he supported all societies for Korean revolution against Japan. Most of his relations had moved out of Korea since the Japanese occupation—into Manchuria and Russia—but Pak still lived believing that the time must come to go

Students at a flying school in Redwood City, California, in 1919.

back, and even now, with a little money sent in care of a brother-in-law, he had bought a minute piece of land to the north of Seoul. For fifteen years his single ambition had been to get back there and settle down. On Korean land, he wanted to raise 100 percent Korean children, who would be just as patriotic as himself. . . .

Another character in the novel, Chungpa Han, offers to read the newspaper to Pak, but Pak is "only interested to know what had happened in the Korean revolution, which had already quieted down. At least in the American newspapers."

Chungpa Han does not share Pak's patriotic zeal. Han says, "It was as if I saw Korea receding farther and farther from me." Han feels lonely in the Korean community, where the homeland is always kept before the immigrants' eyes. Still, Han sees that Pak and the other nationalists have a country and an identity, while he seems to have neither. He thinks that he has been westernized and cannot go home, back to Korea, except for a "visit."

But as a Korean, Han feels unwelcome in America. He is told by an American senator: "Young man, I can see you have come to America to stay, and I'm proud and glad. Now you must definitely make up your mind to *be* American. Don't say, 'I'm Korean' when you're asked. Say 'I'm an American.'" Han realizes that the senator has no understanding of his plight as an Asian immigrant. He tells the senator, "But an Oriental has a hard time in America. He is not welcome much." The senator does not listen to Han's explanation; instead he loudly insists, "There shouldn't be any buts about it! Believe in America with all your heart. . . . I tell you, sir, you belong here. You should be one of us." And Han tries again, reminding the senator that he cannot even become a citizen: "But legally I am denied."

Han feels apart both from the land of his birth and from the land where he now lives. This sense of separateness haunts him in a dream he has over and over. In this dream, Han climbs a tree and sees a "hairlike bridge" stretching across the ocean to Korea. "Creeping across this bridge and beckoning with eyes of glee" are Yunkoo and Chak-soo-shay—the boys he had played with as a child. Then he sees at the other end of the bridge "a paradise of wild and flowery magic, with mountains and waterfalls and little gushing streams." Han struggles to reach the bridge as he hears Yunkoo and Chak-soo-shay daring him to follow them. They are "standing up now and running back and forth like men on a tightrope across the little trembling bridge." Han almost reaches the bridge. But suddenly, things begin tumbling out of his pockets, "money and keys, contracts and business letters." One of the things that falls out is the key to Han's American car. Sliding down the tree, Han scrabbles among the leaves and sticks on the ground, anxiously looking for the car key. He cannot find the key, the symbol of American success, and the dream ends with Han looking out through iron bars at a terrifying mob of red-faced men with clubs and knives, shouting "fire, bring fire." The character of Han, lost and afraid of racial violence, is Younghill Kang's symbol of the Koreans who felt lost between two worlds, separated forever from their ancestral homeland yet unable to belong fully to America.

Korean American children found themselves pulled in two directions: their parents urged them to cling to their identity as Koreans, yet the young people felt an overwhelming desire to be "American."

LIKE YOUNGHILL KANG'S FICTIONAL CHARACTER
Chungpa Han, many second-generation Koreans also found
themselves floating "insecurely, in the rootless groping fash-
ion of men hung between two worlds." They did not share
the fierce patriotism of their immigrant parents. Indeed, in
the eyes of many immigrant Koreans, the second generation
was a problem. Korean young people born in America were
"hyphenized Koreans." They had "very little knowledge of
and appreciation for their ancestral connections." They did
not seem to care about their Korean roots. "To them only
the glimmer and comforts of American life appeal; nothing
else matters," older Koreans complained about the second
generation.

The immigrants tried hard to keep love for the homeland alive in their children. In his advice to his children and
grandchildren, Sa-sun Whang, who had fled Korea as a political refugee, said, "Keep your Koreanness. Don't lose your
Korean spirit. Even though you are an American citizen, you
have to remember our ancestors, our people. I don't want my
children's children to forget their own country. Even though
they weren't born there, or don't know the history or customs,
I want them to keep the Korean spirit."

But second-generation Koreans found that it was not
easy to keep something they had never had. Jean Park, who
grew up in the agricultural country of the San Joaquin Valley
of central California, shared the experiences of young Koreans
in America. Her story shows what it meant to grow up Korean
American.

As a child, Jean Park noticed that the small town
where she lived was "predominantly Caucasian and Caucasians ran the town." There was a main street with "one big

A young Korean family in Ohio in the 1920s adapts to American ways.

general store and a couple of other shops that were operated by Caucasians." Years later, she recalled, "At that time, we were the only Orientals living in Taft. There were a few Mexicans . . . and they were looked down upon. The Caucasians used to call them 'Wetbacks.'" Jean and her brother and sister played together all of the time, for "nobody ever came by our house to call us out to play." When Jean and her family went to town, they became the targets of stares, as though they were "criminals or something." The Caucasian children laughed and made faces at them.

The Park family's encounters with whites were not always negative. "One day I came home from school and found the Caucasian widow, who lived across the street, crying on my mother's shoulder," recalled Jean. "She had injured herself seriously and one of her daughters had died in an automobile accident. This lady was a warm-hearted person and she treated us like her family. The incident stands out in my memory because it was the only time that a Caucasian person had come to us for sympathy."

Like most of the workers in town, Jean's father was employed by the Standard Oil Company. "Though I never heard him speak English in our home, I remember he used English when he spoke with Caucasians," she said. "He must have learned English from the missionaries in Korea." Her father was at least 20 years older than her mother. Jean's mother did all the housework, raised the children, and also did laundry for whites. She was extremely resourceful. Before she learned English, she figured out how to ask for what she needed. One day her white landlord asked her whether she needed anything at the grocery store. Explained Jean's mother: "I didn't know how to say 'egg,' so I crumpled a white handkerchief into a ball and I then imitated a chicken laying an egg. I moved my arms like a chicken and I made noises like a chicken. Then I tried to get some beef; so I imitated a cow who went 'moo-oo.'"

Jean's mother was a Korean nationalist who constantly talked about "her hope for Korea's freedom from Japan," Jean said. "She devoted what time she had to Korea's fight for independence and even gave some of her savings to the movement. Her life-long ambition was to return to a free Korea." She loved Korean songs, and would often sing:

Ari-rang, Ari-rang, A-ra-ri-yo
He is going over the Ari-rang Hill
Since he leaves me all alone
He'll have a pain in his foot without going very far.

She taught her children how to speak, read, and write Korean, and she also introduced them to Korean customs. "Many of the books we used came from Korea," Jean remembered, "and some of the books were borrowed from other Koreans. My mother was very strict. We had to memorize everything perfectly. She taught us the numbers, 'hanna, tul, saette' . . . and the alphabets and we repeated after her."

Korean bachelors from nearby towns often visited Jean's family. They sat around with her parents, always talking about Korea. One of these visitors, named Kim, was a sort of uncle to Jean and her siblings. "In his old black limousine that looked like a hearse," Jean lovingly recounted, "he would drive us everywhere. Sometimes he drove us to nearby towns and other times we went to the mountains. When he drove us to town he treated us to ice-cream, soda, and candy." They would take hikes in the mountains, and he would chase the children up and down the hills. "He was very generous and loved children even though he didn't have kids of his own," said Jean. Like many immigrant men, Kim had no family of his own and so he treasured the moments spent with the Park family.

At an early age, Jean realized that her parents preferred sons to daughters. She said, "My father expected a boy but instead I was born. I felt sorry for my father and I tried hard

Taken in either Dinuba or Reedley, California, around 1912, this photograph reflects the presence of a Korean community in and around the towns where Jean Park grew up.

to please him whenever I could." She also found that her mother "favored boys over girls too because when she had her next child, a son, she rejoiced happily. She even went out of her way to make my brother happy. Though she did little things for my brother, I noticed them."

Jean never forgot the summer afternoon her father charged through the door of their house cursing in Korean. Jean knew something was wrong because he had never come home so early. "What happened? Why did you come home from work?" her mother asked apprehensively. "I'm fired!" he exploded. Jean overheard her father say that a "jealous Caucasian" did not like him because he was "Oriental." This man had urged the supervisor to fire him.

After Jean's father was fired, her mother "became the dominant one in the family. She wore the pants in the family and made all of the important decisions. My father and the rest of us listened to everything she told us to do." She decided to raise chickens, and the family built a large chicken coop for 500 chicks. "The business prospered well for a few months," Jean said. "Then I remember we woke up one morning to feed the chickens but when we got to the chicken coop the fences were ripped apart." Most of the chickens were gone. Angrily the Parks drove toward town. On the way they saw a truck with two white men in the front and chickens in the back. "We stared at them suspiciously but then we drove on," Jean said. "My mother and father were so upset they didn't stop the men in the truck but I knew they were the ones who stole our chickens and ruined the chicken coop. For a long time I remembered their faces. After this incident the whole family took a dislike to Caucasians and we never associated with them until we moved to Reedley."

Reedley was a small town on the eastern edge of the valley. It had a main street with two theaters, gas stations, and some grocery and hardware stores. "The people in Reedley lived segregated according to race," Jean noticed. "One race lived in one section of town and another race lived in another section." There were Mexicans, Japanese, Chinese, Koreans, Germans, and Italians. "Most of the Chinese had private businesses like grocery stores and restaurants. They formed a tightly knit community of their own residing mainly in one section of the town." The Japanese also had their own little community of Japanese grocery stores, ice cream shops, barbershops, and hardware stores.

The Korean community was small at first: "There were ten to twelve Korean families who lived a mile or two apart from each other. Most of the Korean families worked as farm workers and they barely made a living." This community grew as Koreans came to Reedley from Colorado, Montana, Oregon, and Washington. Said Jean, "Every year the Korean community got bigger and bigger until there were at least a hundred or two hundred."

Racial and ethnic boundaries were drawn sharply in Reedley. German parents never allowed their children to play with Koreans. Whenever Jean and other Korean children walked through the German neighborhood, the children stared and made faces at them. "On the whole the Japanese looked down upon the Koreans," Jean recalled. "They felt superior to us. Rarely was there a Japanese boy or girl who treated a Korean boy or girl equally."

But people sometimes crossed these ethnic lines. Jean explained, "Most of the Japanese knew us well because my mother spoke Japanese fluently. Although we were poor the

Japanese grocers gave us charge accounts because they all knew my mother." Jean and her family also found the Italian families "very friendly." The Italian families, like the Koreans, lived on "the poor side of town," and Jean's family became good friends with the Buccis, who had recently immigrated from Italy.

In Reedley, Jean's father worked as a farm laborer. He made very little money, and the family faced financial hardships. Poverty among the Koreans created a sense of community as they reached out to each other for support. Jean remembered that one Korean family helped the others. She said, "One thing I'll never forget about the Lees is that they were very understanding and they always helped other Koreans. If ever a Korean needed financial or other help the Lees were the first to volunteer. I guess they lived such a hard life themselves that they were always willing to lend a helping hand."

Reedley did not have a Korean church, so the Parks and other Koreans traveled on Sundays to the Korean church in the nearby town of Dinuba to worship and socialize. The minister was from Korea. When he prayed, "he rocked up and down on the balls of his feet. . . . He baptised my brother, sister, and me at a nearby river in Dinuba. He dunked my head below the surface of the water and chanted a prayer. Meanwhile I must have swallowed at least a cup of water. I didn't like being christened at all." Later the Kim Brothers—the agriculturalists who invented the nectarine—gave money to build a big church for the Koreans in Reedley.

Jean's family moved from Reedley to Sanger, then back to Reedley. "Like my family, most of the the Koreans were poor and they had to move a lot so that they could

A family portrait. In the 1930s and 1940s, Korean American families like this one were much more numerous in the western states than elsewhere in the country.

Close ties among family members and friends provided a comforting antidote to the racism and prejudice that was all too often encountered by Jean Park and other Korean Americans.

improve their socio-economic status," she explained. "There was no choice. They had to keep moving until they could get firmly established."

During this time, Jean's mother made some money by selling homemade liquor. She invested the money in a trucking business, shipping fruit and vegetables from farms in the San Joaquin Valley to the produce markets in Los Angeles. Meanwhile, Jean's father was drinking heavily. He became ill and had to go to the hospital, and his medical bills ate up the family's savings. Tragedy followed. Said Jean, "One day we woke up and found my father hanging from the tree. He hung himself. After that night our dog howled every day at night and it bothered us because it reminded us of the hanging so we had to shoot the dog."

Jean remembered her mother's grief. She also remembered that a white neighbor woman "came over every day to bring back my mother's faith. She was an understanding lady. Every single day she cooked food for my mother and saw to it that my mother gained her strength back. 'Now you have a family to take care of,' she told my mother. 'So you can't let this upset you. You've got to take care of all your children.'" Jean's mother recovered, only to face the economic troubles of the Great Depression of the 1930s. She had to depend on welfare and worked as a farm laborer whenever she could.

At school in the San Joaquin Valley, Jean and other Korean children felt like strangers among the white children and teachers. "It took me several months before I could understand the English language and my teacher," Jean said. "Whenever my teacher said anything to me I just nodded my head and pretended as if I knew what she said. Most of the children ignored me in school until I began to pick up the English language; so I was a loner in the beginning. I felt out of place because wherever I turned I saw kids with blonde hair and blue eyes." Jean and her sister wore dresses, and her brother wore blue jeans, and they all tried to look American. "During lunchtime we ate in the school cafeteria since my mother felt that it would embarrass us to take rice and kimchee." They were afraid the white children would call them "hot pepper eaters and garlic eaters."

But gradually Jean and other Korean children developed friendships with Italian, Portuguese, Mexican, and even Japanese children. "I was lucky," Jean said, pointing out that some Japanese were prejudiced against Koreans, "because I found a Japanese girl friend who was very nice and we got along well." Another girl, an Italian American, was the same age as Jean, and the two became best friends. In the spring the two friends had fun picking berries and mushrooms at a nearby river. "We practically lived at each other's homes," said Jean. One of her brother's close friends was a Mexican boy. The children of different ethnic groups would go swimming together in the river and attended vacation bible school together. In junior high school, they went to dances. "Sometimes we drove up to Visalia on Fridays," said Jean, "because Chinese boys held dances there." Despite her mother's insistence that she date only Korean boys, Jean's sister had Japanese boyfriends, and she also dated a Mexican boy and an Italian boy.

Growing up in America, second-generation Koreans seemed to drift away from the intense nationalism of their

Twin sisters from Korea become U.S. citizens at a naturalization ceremony in Detroit in 1987.

parents. "My mother got involved in Korean politics and she was a real patriot," Jean recalled. "All of the first generation Koreans joined the independence movement. . . . Most of us second generation Koreans didn't join the independence movement but we just watched all the elderly Koreans."

Jean Park and most of her fellow second-generation Koreans stayed on the sidelines. They had not even been to Korea. The loss of the homeland and the indignity of Japanese domination were not as painful to them as to their parents. The Korean American generation did not hate the Japanese; in school and on the playground, young Korean Americans even had Japanese friends. They did not sadly see themselves as drifting people, exiles from their homeland, the way the first generation of immigrants did.

Young Korean Americans saw a widening gap between the two generations. The "elders tried to influence the children with their native customs and ideas," but the younger generation "took to an American idea rapidly." A Korean youth said, "By law I am American and by heart I am American, although I am not of the same color or race." They heard their parents talking about the struggle for Korean independence, but they did not "pay any attention to it." They read community newspapers like the *New Korea,* but "the news in the paper had little significance to them."

One young Korean American expressed the feelings of many of the immigrants' children: "So far I have read very little about my parents' native land. I have never felt a sense of pride in knowing about my parents' native land but I have pity and sympathy for them." For the second-generation Koreans, the future was in America, not Korea.

Lieutenant Young Kim of Los Angeles receives the Silver Star for gallantry in action during World War II in Italy. Korean Americans served in the U.S. armed forces not just as regular troops but also as intelligence experts and translators.

BY 1941, WORLD WAR II WAS RAGING IN EUROPE AND also in Asia, where Japan had invaded China. The United States, however, had not entered the war. On the morning of December 7, several Koreans in Los Angeles were rehearsing for a play sponsored by the Society for Aid to the Korean Volunteer Corps in China. They wanted to raise money to help 200,000 refugee Korean families living in China and also to support Korean volunteers who were fighting the Japanese. The rehearsal was suddenly interrupted by an electrifying announcement: "The Japanese have attacked Pearl Harbor." At once, everyone on the stage cried, *Taehan toknip manse!"* ("Long live Korean independence!")

One of the players, Bong-Youn Choy, later recalled, "No Korean, old and young alike, could control his emotions of joy. Every Korean felt that the long dream for national independence would soon become a reality." The bombing of Pearl Harbor, an American naval base in Hawaii, meant that the United States would enter the war against Japan. Koreans in the United States, especially first-generation immigrants who still felt strong ties to their homeland, hoped that the war would drive the Japanese out of Korea, which they had held for nearly 40 years.

That night, Koreans gathered at the Korean National Association in Los Angeles to discuss how they would act during the war. They would make every effort to contribute to the American war effort. Those who were able would volunteer for the national guard; others would buy war bonds; still others would offer their skills—for example, Koreans who spoke Japanese could help the U.S. armed forces by serving as translators and interpreters.

Some Korean nationalists welcomed the war, hoping that the United States and its allies would crush Japan and bring about Korean independence. But for many Koreans in America the war years were a time of painful confusion. They watched with mixed feelings as their Japanese American neighbors, many of whom had been born in the United States, were treated as spies and enemy agents. Among white Americans, anti-Japanese feeling reached its peak in February 1942, when President Franklin D. Roosevelt ordered all people of Japanese descent in California, Oregon, and Washington to be interned, or placed in guarded camps, during the war. The order affected 110,000 people on the West Coast, 70,000 of whom were U.S. citizens. Forced to sell or abandon their homes and businesses at short notice, many of them lost everything but the few possessions they could carry with them. They were taken to internment camps where they lived like convicted criminals, surrounded by barbed wire and armed guards.

"When World War Two broke out," Jean Park remembered, "we were still living in Reedley." A few months after the attack on Pearl Harbor, she began to hear stories that the Japanese were being taken to the camps. "People said that the Japanese were treated very cruelly and that they were dragged to unknown destinations," she recalled. When the Japanese were taken to the internment camps, opportunities opened up for Koreans. For example, Jean Park's stepfather moved the family to southern California where "the Japanese lost all their farms and many of the farms were being sold for very cheap prices."

But when Jean and her family arrived at their new home, they found whites staring at them and shouting, "Japs

go home!" Like many other Korean Americans, the Parks had been mistaken for Japanese. Said Jean of the townspeople, "They were ready to stone us with rocks and descend on us because they had that evil look in their eyes." To protect themselves from anti-Japanese violence, Koreans wore badges with the Korean flag or the statement "I am a Korean." They also put similar stickers on their cars.

Koreans in America, protesting decades of Japanese occupation of Korea, made their anti-Japanese views clear.

Even the U.S. government sometimes failed to distinguish the Koreans from the Japanese. Because Japan controlled Korea, a 1940 U.S. law identified Korean immigrants as subjects of Japan. In 1941, after the United States declared war against Japan, the American government identified Koreans in the United States as "enemy aliens." In February 1942, the *Korean National Herald–Pacific Weekly* insisted that the government identify Koreans as Koreans. "The Korean is an enemy of Japan," the paper declared. "Since December 7, the Korean here is between the devil and the deep sea for the reason that the United States considers him a subject of Japan, which the Korean resents as an injustice to his true status. . . . What is the status of a Korean in the United States? Is he an enemy alien? Has any Korean ever been in Japanese espionage or in subversive activities against the land where he makes his home and rears his children as true Americans?"

In Hawaii, Koreans were also classified as enemy aliens. Korean immigrants who worked on defense projects in the islands experienced an even more painful insult: they were classified as Japanese and had to wear black-bordered badges showing this status. "For years we've been fighting the Japanese and now they tell us that we're Japs. It's an insult!" Koreans snapped angrily. "It's an insult!" "Why in the hell do they pull a trick like this on us," the Korean workers screamed, "when we hate the Japanese more than anyone else in the world." After their protests, they were only allowed to add the words "I am Korean" to their badges.

Some young Koreans, however, sympathized with the Japanese Americans on the West Coast, who lost their homes and jobs when they were interned in the camps. "It made me feel sad to hear that their land was taken away from them," said Jean Park, "and that they were imprisoned." Second-generation Koreans in Hawaii did not see the local Japanese as the enemy. A young Korean man explained that the bombing of Pearl Harbor did not make him feel any differently toward his Japanese neighbors and acquaintances. "We've lived with them all along and know them well and it didn't occur to me that they were responsible," he said.

Some Korean nationalists viewed the matter in a more sinister light. One Korean nationalist leader declared early in 1941 that 35,000 to 50,000 Japanese in Hawaii were ready to help Japan in a war against the United States; he also urged the U.S. government to intern the Japanese Americans on the West Coast, claiming that they were spying for Japan. He said, "It is our conviction that the best way to prepare against the Japanese is to let the American people know the Japanese plans and what the Japs and the Japanese Americans are doing in this country."

Korean immigrants were eager to contribute to the American war effort against Japan. Many Koreans possessed an invaluable weapon that the country needed: they knew the Japanese language. During the war, they taught Japanese to American soldiers and translated captured Japanese documents. They also made radio broadcasts in Japanese to undermine support for Japan in the Pacific nations, and they served as secret agents in parts of Asia that were occupied by Japanese forces.

In Los Angeles, 109 Koreans—one-fifth of the city's Korean population—joined the California National Guard. Ranging in ages from 18 to 65, they were organized into a Korean unit called the Tiger Brigade. They drilled regularly on Saturday and Sunday afternoons in Exposition Park, pre-

To Koreans in the United States and around the world, the war in Asia offered the hope that Korea might be liberated from Japanese domination. Their enmity toward Japan made it especially galling when white Americans confused them with the Japanese.

paring to defend California against an enemy invasion. A white army officer congratulated the men of the Tiger Brigade, saying, "I myself have learned the real meaning of patriotism during my participation in this Tiger Brigade, and I cannot find adequate words to describe your contribution in winning this war." Elderly Koreans, too, made their contributions, the women serving in the Red Cross and the men volunteering as emergency fire wardens. Koreans in Hawaii

and on the U.S. mainland bought defense bonds to help pay for the war effort. In 1942–43, they bought more than $239,000 worth of bonds—an immense sum for a population of only 10,000 people.

All of this involvement in the war effort earned the Koreans new respect from white Americans. At the celebration of the Korean National Flag Day on August 29, 1943, the mayor of Los Angeles raised the Korean flag to honor the uniformed men of the Tiger Brigade as they marched past City Hall. A year later, a congressional delegate from Hawaii tried to get Congress to pass a law that would allow Korean immigrants to become naturalized American citizens. He failed, however; the United States was not yet ready to grant citizenship to Asian immigrants. But the fact that he had tried was proof that Koreans were gaining greater acceptance in American society.

As the Koreans in America had hoped, World War II did bring about the end of Japanese rule in Korea, although not in the way that the Korean patriots had expected. Korea was liberated by United States forces who entered from the south and Soviet forces who entered from the north. Each of these superpowers had its own ideas about the kind of government that should be established in Korea, so the country was divided into two parts. North Korea, or the Democratic People's Republic of Korea, became a communist state supported by its powerful communist neighbors, the Soviet Union and the People's Republic of China. South Korea, called the Republic of Korea, was backed by the United States. This division of Korea into two zones administered by foreign powers was a sad blow to Koreans who had hoped that their country would become fully independent as soon as the war ended.

In 1950, North Korea and South Korea went to war with each other. The United States sent troops to reinforce South Korea's armed forces, while the People's Republic of China entered the war on the side of North Korea. By the time the two sides signed a peace agreement in 1953, more than a million Koreans on both sides had been killed.

Koreans in America had mixed feelings about the Korean War. As they watched events unfold in their homeland, they were saddened to see "Koreans killing Koreans." Some of them supported North Korea, some supported South Korea, but all feared that the war would not lead to the reunification of the country.

The Korean War doubled the size of the Korean population in the United States. Before the war, there were about 10,000 Koreans in Hawaii and the mainland. These were the original immigrants from the early years of the century, the picture brides who had arrived a few years later, and their descendants, as well as a few hundred 'students, diplomats, and political exiles. But from 1950 to 1964, approximately 14,000 new Korean immigrants entered the United States as the wives or adopted children of American citizens. Many of them were war brides—Korean women who had married U.S. servicemen stationed in Korea. Some were the children of American servicemen and Korean women; others were Korean children who had been orphaned in the war and were adopted by American families.

Even with these newcomers, the Korean population in America was still quite small in the mid-1960s. The Korean Americans were a hidden minority. These few Koreans in the

United States were spread out geographically, not concentrated in large ethnic communities such as San Francisco's Chinatown. Many white Americans were barely aware of the Koreans among them. But in the mid-1960s, a new wave of Asian immigration would bring sweeping changes to the Korean population of the United States. Koreans would become a highly visible part of multicultural America.

California was the main point of entry for the first wave of immigrants from Korea, but many who came after 1965—in the age of easy air travel—arrived in New York, which soon had a large Korean community.

Chapter Seven

The Second Wave of Korean Immigration

IN 1965, THE U.S. CONGRESS PASSED A NEW FEDERAL immigration law that opened the door to immigrants from Asia—a door that had been slammed shut by the immigration law of 1924. This new immigration law grew out of the achievements of the civil rights movement, which had been struggling to eliminate racism from American society.

The civil rights movement had begun to awaken America's moral conscience. African Americans—and progressive whites—launched massive protests against racial discrimination and segregation. In 1954, the U.S. Supreme Court declared that racially segregated schools were unconstitutional. Ten years later, after countless civil rights protests and marches led by Martin Luther King and others, Congress passed the Civil Rights Act of 1964, outlawing racial discrimination. The next step was to extend the idea of equality to the people who were seeking to enter the United States. "Everywhere else in our national life, we have eliminated discrimination based on national origins," argued Robert Kennedy, attorney general of the United States. "Yet, this system is still the foundation of our immigration law." But the African American struggle for civil rights had set the wheels of change in motion. A year after the Civil Rights Act was passed, Congress passed a new immigration law that did not discriminate on the basis of race or national origin.

The 1965 immigration law allowed 20,000 people from each Asian country to enter the United States each year. After living in the United States for five years, they could become naturalized citizens. Then they could sponsor the immigration of their spouses, children, parents, and brothers and sisters, who in turn could become citizens and send for their own relatives and in-laws. In this way large extended

Korean American children—some in traditional Korean dress, others in all-American blue jeans—play at an Asian arts festival. Asian Americans today seek to celebrate their Asian cultures without lessening their claim to be full members of American society.

families have been able to come to America from Asian countries, including Korea.

The Korean population in the United States began growing, both in the total number of Korean Americans and also in how Koreans compared with other Asian American groups. In 1960, only 1% of all Asian Americans were Korean. By 1985, 11% were Korean.

This second wave of immigration made Koreans much more visible in America. For decades, the Korean population in Hawaii and the U.S. mainland had been around 10,000. Between 1965 and 1985, it jumped to half a million. By the beginning of the 1990s, more than 100,000 Koreans were living in New York, where a cluster of Korean restaurants and stores had appeared on Broadway between 23rd and 31st streets. Los Angeles County was the home of 200,000 Koreans. A new community had sprung up along Olympic Boulevard in Los Angeles: "It's called Koreatown," *Newsweek* magazine reported in 1975. "What used to be Mexican-American, Japanese and Jewish stores and businesses are now mostly Korean, with giant Oriental letters spread across their low-slung storefronts." This concentration of Korean-owned grocery stores, churches, gas stations, travel agencies, barbershops, insurance companies, restaurants, and nightclubs caused one Korean immigrant to say, "One does not feel that one lives in America when one lives on Olympic Boulevard."

Most of the recent Korean immigrants have been from the college-educated middle class rather than from the farming and working classes. Surveys of Korean householders in New York and Los Angeles have found that about 70% of them had college degrees when they arrived in the United States. Many of them had been professional and technical workers in Korea. Unlike the first-wave immigrants who left Korea as temporary laborers, planning to return, the new immigrants have come to America as permanent settlers, bringing their families with them. A majority of them have applied for citizenship when they meet the five-year residence requirement. "The fascination of America for the Korean immigrants," said one immigrant in 1975, "is to come to a free and abundant country, and breathe in its air of freedom, and make plans for a new life such that they are changing their destinies, which were fatalistically determined by tradition and history in the old country."

The U.S. immigration law of 1965 made it possible for large numbers of Koreans to enter the United States at a time of rapid economic and social change in Korea. In the 1960s and 1970s, South Korea developed modern industries to produce goods, including clothing and electronic equipment, to be sold in other countries. To keep the prices of Korean goods low enough that other countries would buy them, industries paid their workers low wages. The government helped keep down wages by outlawing labor strikes. The Korean government also held down the price of rice, which meant that many farmers could not make enough money from the land. The farmers then had to come to the cities to look for factory jobs. Millions of Koreans flowed from the countryside into the cities, which became overcrowded. At the same time, South Korea was having a population explosion, making the overcrowding even worse. "Korea's population density is one of the world's highest," explained an official of a Korean bank in California in 1976, "so the natural tendency is to seek some better opportunity than at home where competition is too keen." For many Koreans, that "better opportunity" seemed to be the United States.

Seoul and other Korean cities simply did not have enough jobs—especially for educated professional and technical workers. Thousands of professionals began leaving Korea and going to Germany, Brazil, Argentina, Canada, and the United States. "I could not find a job after obtaining my B.S. in chemical engineering at Chungnam University," said one man. He applied for an overseas labor contract and worked in Germany as a miner for three years. "I was afraid that I would become unemployed again if I returned to the home country," he said. "I wandered through some European nations for a while, but I could not find a proper place to settle. Upon arriving in the United States, I found a lot of jobs waiting for me."

There have been many medical professionals among the recent Korean immigrants. For example, between 1965 and 1977, more than 13,000 Korean physicians, nurses, pharmacists, and dentists entered the United States. South Korea's modern new medical training schools have produced more graduates than the country could employ—in 1973, nearly three-fifths of the nurses who graduated from training school in Korea could not find jobs. "The schools in Korea produce many qualified doctors," said a Korean immigrant who sponsored the immigration of his brother and sister, both doctors. "The truth is they have more doctors in Korea than they can support—not more than they need, but American cities can use more too." Unable to find jobs in the major cities and unwilling to go into rural areas with low profits and low standards of living, many Korean doctors left Korea for the United States.

Arriving in the United States, Korean nurses and physicians have been drawn to the East Coast, where there has been a shortage of medical workers. In 1980, one-fourth to one-fifth of all Korean immigrant nurses and doctors were working in New York City. "Korean doctors of New York," a Korean American sociologist observed, "are the most 'successful' of Korean immigrants. They represent the largest group of Korean suburban houseowners; most of the Korean residents of Scarsdale are immigrant doctors. With MD plates on their cars, the Korean doctors in New York can display their highly esteemed status in white suburban neighborhoods."

But the appearance of high status conceals some frustrating realities. Korean doctors have often found themselves confined to inner-city hospitals and shunned by white doctors. They tend to find jobs in fields such as anesthesiology and radiology instead of high-status fields such as surgery and internal medicine. Beginning in the late 1970s, Korean doctors also saw a drop in the demand for physicians and a new wave of discrimination against foreign doctors when they applied for positions in hospitals.

Many Korean doctors have not even been able to practice medicine in the United States. They discovered they simply could not support a family and also prepare for the many tests they had to take, including an English language test and an examination in their special medical field. As a result, some Korean doctors, especially those with limited English language skills, have been working as hospital orderlies and nurses' assistants.

Korean pharmacists, too, have had trouble practicing their professions in the United States. In California, for example, Korean pharmacists cannot even take the state licensing test because the board that administers the test does not include Korean pharmacy schools on its list of approved schools. Seung Sook Myung's story is typical. She had been a pharmacist in Korea for 10 years before coming to Los Angeles in 1974. Because she was not able to take the state licensing examination, she could not work as a pharmacist in her new home. She became a knitting machine operator at a plant where nine out of ten workers were Korean. Like many other educated, professional Korean immigrants, Myung found herself locked into low-wage work.

Kong Mook Lee, another pharmacist who immigrated to Los Angeles, invested his money in a garment factory when he found that he could not practice pharmacy. "The only thing my wife knows is sewing," he said. "The only thing I know is pharmacy. Pharmacy is impossible; so sewing is the only way." Lee counted at least 300 experienced Korean pharmacists in southern California alone who had to change occupations. "We never expected to lose our profession at the same time as we immigrated to this beautiful and wonderful country," he said. "Today, most of us find ourselves in a job which is inconsistent with our qualification and experience. We are suffering from starvation wages."

Korean teachers and business administrators have also found limited job prospects in America. In fact, many Korean professionals in the United States are underemployed—that is, they work at jobs belows their level of training and education. A survey in Los Angeles in 1978 found that only about one-third of professional immigrants were able to find professional jobs in the United States. Korean immigrants who were office workers in their home country have become auto mechanics, welders, radio and television repairpersons, gas-station attendants, gardeners, and janitors in America.

For many Koreans, the answer to job discrimination and downgrading has been self-employment. They have opened their own small businesses, such as wig shops, restaurants, liquor stores, and especially greengroceries (stores that sell fruit and vegetables). A writer in the *New York Times* observed that greengroceries have long been run by immi-

A sweatshop, where clothing is produced for the garment industry. Many recent immigrants, especially women, find their opportunities limited to low-paying jobs under substandard working conditions.

grants: "In fruits and vegetables, traditionally an immigrant business, first it was Jews . . . then Italians. And now up in the Bronx, it's the Koreans."

By 1983, Koreans dominated the produce business, owning three-quarters of the greengroceries in New York City. Korean greengrocers have become so numerous that they compete with one another. "Across the street from me," remarked the new owner of a store in the South Bronx, "there is another Korean greengrocer; he bought his place from a Chinese four years ago. One block down, there's another Korean: he got his store from an old Jewish man who moved to Florida. Across from him, there's still another Korean. . . . Four Korean greengrocers in this crowded ghetto area!"

Because they have a very high rate of self-employment, the Korean newcomers are sometimes praised for their ethnic enterprise. But Korean ethnic enterprise in America is the result of complex circumstances. The new Korean immigrants were not shopkeepers in Korea. A survey in New York in the mid-1970s showed that only 6% of Korean householders had owned small businesses in the old country, yet more than a third of them were small-business operators in New York.

Some of these immigrants obtained money to open their businesses from small Korean cooperative credit associations. But they have also gotten loans from the Small Business Administration. Most important, however, they brought money with them, unlike the first wave of Korean immigrants. Beginning in 1981, Koreans have been allowed by the South Korean government to take up to $100,000 out of the country. Many immigrants bring with them the money to start a business in America.

In addition, the Korean newcomers have become shopkeepers at a crucial time in the history of American cities. Middle-class whites have been fleeing to the suburbs, abandoning the inner cities to blacks and Latinos. Older white merchants have been closing their businesses to retreat from the growing ghetto or to retire. "Before the Korean immigrants landed in this city, who were the greengrocers?" said Eugene Kang of New York's Korean Produce Association. "Most likely, they were Jewish and Italian, along with Greeks. The Jews and Italians and Greeks, they are third generation now. They want to go to law school. They are no longer taking care of father's business, which was greengrocer." These changes in the cities opened a place in the economy for Koreans. To many immigrants, however, it seems strange and ironic that they left professional jobs in modernized, industrialized South Korea to become old-fashioned shopkeepers in America.

Many Korean immigrants have felt pushed into self-employment. "What else can I do?" asked a greengrocer who has a master's degree in city planning and mechanical engineering. "I need money but there are not good jobs for Koreans." A majority of Korean small-business operators are college graduates; nearly four-fifths of the Korean greengrocers in New York have college degrees. Unable to find professional jobs, they would rather work for themselves than work as low-paid laborers.

The dream of many immigrants continues to be self-employment. Korean delicatessens and restaurants, often offering a wide variety of food for take-out meals, are now a familiar feature of many cities.

The language barrier is another reason Koreans have turned to shopkeeping. Many of them have limited English language skills, which means that professional jobs are beyond their reach. "The language barrier," observed Ha Tai Kim, "virtually makes the newcomers deaf and dumb." Working long hours to make ends meet, most Koreans do not have time for English classes. But they can get by in greengroceries and other small businesses with only a limited knowledge of English.

Racial discrimination has also driven Koreans into shopkeeping. "When it comes to getting employment in American firms, factories, public and private institutions," charged Ha Tai Kim, "there is a great deal of difficulty in securing jobs due to discrimination and language barriers." Explaining why he resigned from a New York insurance company and became a greengrocer, a man who has a master of business administration degree from an American university said, "When I began to work for the insurance company, I met an Asian co-worker. This man had been with the company for several years. He was born in the U.S. His English was perfect. He was a hard worker. But he received only token promotions and was regularly bypassed by the white American workers who joined the firm after he did. I thought, 'This guy is good. But if he's not making it, neither will I.' So I left. In the store, at least, I'm in control of my own future."

Many Korean shopkeepers rely entirely on their families to operate their businesses. Korean immigrant women generally speak little or no English. Their job prospects in the general labor market have been very limited. But they are a source of unpaid labor for their husbands who own small shops. In a Korean-owned family business, everyone works.

The workday for Korean shopkeepers and their families begins early in the morning. A newspaper article described a typical day in the life of a Korean greengrocer in New York City: "Mr. Kim bought his store two years ago from a Jewish American for a total payment of $15,000—$10,000 for the store price and $5,000 in key money. He and his son daily purchase vegetables: at four o'clock every morning when the dawn is coming, they get up and drive to Hunts Point in the Bronx, where a city-run wholesale market is located. . . . In the market they run and run in order to buy at low prices as many as one hundred and seventy different kinds of vegetables and fruits. All the transactions are made in cash. At 7 o'clock they return to the store and mobilize the rest of the family members in order to wash and trim vegetables."

Out on the streets early in the morning darkness and in their stores until late at night, Korean greengrocers sometimes become targets for muggers and armed bandits. Many have been murdered. The physical labor of the business is punishing, too. "No matter how much energy, health, and stamina one may have," many greengrocers say, "one cannot stand more than two years of this daily toil." They complain of backaches and blood in their urine. "Sometimes you get so tired," a greengrocer sighed, "you cannot see the dollar in your hand."

A few greengrocers make handsome profits, clearing more than $100,000 a year. But most of them, for all their hard work and long hours, do not earn very much. The average income from an entire family's labor averages $17,000 to $35,000 a year.

But they work hard, many Korean immigrants say, for their children: "The first generation must be sacrificed." The parents must struggle so that the children can attend college and become professionals as their parents had been in Korea. The parents' lives may have become bleak in the United States, but they will do anything to brighten the futures of their children. In a poem describing the despair he felt for himself and the hope he nurtured for his child, a school janitor who had been a teacher in Korea wrote:

A scene from a play in the traditional Korean style called pansori, *in which actors dramatize and sing versions of popular folk tales to accompaniment provided by a drummer.*

> *I do not see, although I have eyes.*
> *Then, have I become blind? No, I have not.*
> *I do not hear, although I have ears.*
> *Then, have I become deaf? No, I have not.*
> *I do not speak, although I have a mouth.*
> *Then, have I lost my speech? No, I have not.*
> *I have become an old stranger*
> *who wants to raise a young tree*
> *in this wealthy land.*

West and East meet in the world of music: Western-style orchestral performers accompany an artist playing a classical Korean instrument.

Another former teacher in the old country, now a greengrocer, explained the purpose of his work and life: "The day before yesterday I kept my store closed all day long. That was my first day off since I started this business in 1976. My son, Jong Moon, graduated from Princeton University on that day. All my family members came. I am an old man, 65 years. I don't have a driver's license to get to the Hunts Point market. I can't run this business alone. But I have another son to help

through college, Jong Won. I think I can last until both my sons go all the way up, to the highest educational degree."

A Korean lawyer in Los Angeles described the risks and benefits of Korean ethnic enterprise this way: "The immigrants come with a lot of money—$100,000 and $200,000. They sell their homes, everything they own in Korea and bring their cash with them. Many then open liquor stores in the black community. All their transactions are in cash. They are tough. They take risks and know they could get shot by robbers. . . . The Korean businessmen are like the Jews of the 1930s. They are hardworking and aggressive, but because of color they never reach the place where the Jews have reached."

To make their businesses profitable, some Korean business owners hire and exploit other Korean immigrants. They make their employees work long hours, and they pay them low wages, without vacations and health benefits. Korean employers find it easy to hire Korean workers who are desperate for jobs, because these workers are cut off from the mainstream economy by the language barrier and racial discrimination. The plight of these Korean laborers is often overlooked in the newspaper articles and news broadcasts that celebrate the success of Korean shopkeepers. Not all Korean immigrants share in that success. For example, one immigrant woman said that she worked in a garment factory and her husband worked 11 hours a day in a New York fruit and vegetable store owned by another Korean. "We came for a better life," she said wearily, "but we have not found it better yet. It is work, work, work."

Its streets lined with Korean-owned stores and services and thick with signs in the han'gul *alphabet, the Olympic Boulevard district of Los Angeles became the largest Korean community outside Korea.*

WHEN JEAN PARK WAS GROWING UP IN REEDLEY, CALIfornia, there were no large Korean communities. Towns such as Reedley might have a dozen or so Korean families, and there were clusters of Koreans living and working in San Francisco and Los Angeles. But these centers of Korean life in America were quite small, compared with San Francisco's big, bustling Chinatown or Japantown in Seattle. Only in the years after the 1965 immigration law did enough new immigrants arrive in the United States to create big, vibrant Korean communities on the American landscape. In recent decades, Koreans have settled in San Francisco, Oakland, Seattle, Chicago, New York, Washington, D.C., and Anchorage, but the capital of Korean America is in Los Angeles.

Koreans have been present in Los Angeles since the very early days of Korean immigration at the beginning of the 20th century. In 1905, a Korean Presbyterian church was founded on Jefferson Boulevard, near the University of Southern California campus. In the four decades that followed, other Korean churches were established in Los Angeles, as were Korean businesses and community organizations.

Los Angeles was also a center of Korean nationalist movements aimed at freeing Korea from Japanese control. Many Korean nationalist leaders, some of whom had fled their homeland as political refugees, had headquarters in and around Los Angeles. Typical of these was Warren Y. Kim, born Won-yong Kim in Seoul, Korea, in 1896. After joining a resistance group to fight the Japanese, he was forced to flee Korea in 1917. He came to Los Angeles and devoted his energy to studying, working at a variety of jobs, and supporting the Korean cause in California, Hawaii, and South Korea. "I served for many decades for the restoration of Korean independence and I am glad I did," he said. He was one of the founders of the Korean Foundation, established in 1957 to provide financial help to needy Korean students. He also helped start the Korean Center, a meeting place for Korean organizations in Los Angeles, and the Korean Association of Southern California.

The community of Koreans in Los Angeles, never more than a few thousand people, changed after 1965. Los Angeles was one of the main arrival points for immigrants from Korea, and many of them stayed there. They felt that adjusting to life in the United States would be easier in a place where there were people who spoke their language and understood their customs than if they settled in an area with few or no Koreans. As new immigrants came to join friends and family members who had already settled in Los Angeles, that city's Korean population grew dramatically. By 1970, there were nearly 10,000 Koreans in Los Angeles County. In 1975, there were 60,000. By the mid-1970s, Los Angeles had more than 70 Korean Christian churches, a dozen Korean Buddhist temples, more than 100 Korean nonprofit organizations such as youth clubs and business associations, and 1,400 Korean-owned businesses.

The Korean population of southern California continued to increase. By the early 1990s, there were 350,000 Koreans in southern California. Significant Korean communities are present in Garden Grove, Westminster, Gardena, and Cerritos, but more than half of the region's Koreans live in Los Angeles County. Los Angeles contains the biggest Korean community anywhere in the world outside Korea.

Some of the newcomers arrived with enough money to buy stores or start businesses; often this money was their savings from years of working in South Korea or Europe. Others arrived with almost nothing. One of these was Hi-Duk Lee, who immigrated to Los Angeles in 1969 at the age of 29. He had $50 when he arrived. He found work as a welder; his wife worked as a nurse. In three years, they saved $8,000. With that and a loan from a bank, they were able to buy a market and go into business for themselves. Later they used their earnings from the market to open a restaurant and nightclub.

Not all of the immigrants were as successful as Hi-Duk Lee. In 1980 a Korean newspaper in Los Angeles published the life stories of some recent immigrants. Among the accounts were the story of a man who had killed himself because of business debts and another who had died of high blood pressure at age 52. And those who were successful often paid a high price for their achievements. In 1975, the Korean Doctor's Association of Southern California reported that the majority of immigrants were neglecting their health in the struggle for survival. To be profitable, Korean businesses had to stay open long hours and on weekends and holidays. Many Koreans worked for 12 hours or more every day. One woman wrote:

> Dad worked in the gas station 6 A.M. through 12 P.M. at night. I worked 3 P.M. to 7 A.M. Although it was hard and tiring, we thought since we had an opportunity, we ought to work hard. . . . So finally we got the gas station on our own account. We started our own business for the first time. That night my husband and I couldn't sleep. We cried for a long time and promised each other that we would work harder. We didn't even have a bed so we were sleeping on the floor.

A Korean store owner on trial for shooting an African American teenager in 1991. The incident stepped up the growing tension between blacks and Koreans in Los Angeles.

During the 1970s and 1980s, Korean business and cultural life in Los Angeles became centered in a five-square-mile district along Olympic Boulevard. Korean business owners formed their own Korean Chamber of Commerce, and it was this organization that promoted the use of the name "Koreatown" for the Olympic district. The Chamber of Commerce encouraged merchants to put up signs in Korean lettering and helped spread the idea that Koreatown had its own ethnic identity. Once the identity of Koreatown was firmly established, other Korean businesses had even more reason to locate there, and the ethnic character of the neighborhood became even more firmly established.

Koreatown offered both advantages and disadvantages to the immigrants. It was a place where they could express pride in their ethnic heritage and strengthen their ties with one another. Many of the immigrants were newly arrived from Korea and spoke little or no English; for them, Koreatown was a refuge from the confusion of American society. There they could feel at home in a community shaped by the language and customs they had brought with them from Korea.

But this soothing familiarity had a drawback. Many Korean immigrants, especially the older people, were so comfortable in Koreatown that they never ventured outside it. They spoke only Korean, so they had little reason to learn English. Koreatown offered them security, but it also placed limits on their life in the new land. A 1975 article in the *New Korea* newspaper revealed that only 10% of all the Korean immigrants over the age of 23 could speak English fluently. Four out of 10 adult immigrants did not know any English at all. This limited their opportunities for work and education outside the Korean community. A Korean American sociologist observed in 1977, "Korean services and facilities are so plentiful and readily available that a Korean in Los Angeles can, if he chooses, live in a miniature Korea virtually isolated from the mainstream of American society."

As Koreatown continued to grow, the streets became lined with signs in *han'gul*, the Korean alphabet. Along Olympic Boulevard, Western Avenue, Vermont Avenue, and other streets in Koreatown, storefronts that were once rundown or empty became filled with goods being sold by Korean shopkeepers. Liquor stores, greengroceries, restaurants, wig and clothing stores, gas stations, electronics and appliance stores, and food markets, including convenience stores or mini-markets, were among the most popular businesses. Korean lawyers, accountants, travel agents, doctors, dentists, photographers, and insurance and real estate salespersons also offered their services in Koreatown and in a growing number of mini-malls and shopping areas outside Koreatown. Los Angeles had Korean banks, schools teaching traditional Korean dance and martial arts, five Korean newspapers, and Korean television stations.

Some Korean-owned businesses offered products or services especially for Korean customers. Traditional Korean medical services such as herbal medicine and acupuncture, for example, appealed mostly to Koreans, as did grocery stores and restaurants that specialized in Korean delicacies. Many lawyers, physicians, and other professionals conducted business in Korean for the benefit of immigrant clients who did not speak English. Other firms offered lessons in driving or in the English language to newly arrived immigrants.

Yet many of the customers for Korean businesses were white, African American, or Latino. Black and Latino customers were especially numerous, because Koreatown bordered the South Central district of Los Angeles, an inner-city neighborhood where many black and Latino people live. In Koreatown, in South Central, and in other parts of Los Angeles, Korean merchants were brought into daily contact with black and Latino customers.

Tension and conflict sometimes arose between Koreans and members of these ethnic minorities. This was true not just in Los Angeles but in New York and other places where Korean businesses had sprung up in inner-city neighborhoods. People in the black community sometimes resented the Koreans' success. They complained that Korean shopowners did not hire black employees; they also felt that many Koreans treated them disrespectfully. For their part, some Koreans viewed African Americans in terms of unfair stereotypes: blacks were seen as potential robbers or shoplifters.

Each group often misunderstood the other. African Americans who were used to friendly conversation with shopkeepers found many Korean merchants cold and distant, and they felt insulted by what seemed to be unfriendly behavior. They did not realize that in Korean culture it is traditional to show warmth and friendship only to family members and close friends; other people are treated more formally. Steven Shin, who operated a bakery in Los Angeles, explained, "Koreans only smile at very good friends and family, and it's not polite to hug or hold strangers. Blacks complain we don't look them in the eye, but for Koreans to look directly at someone is to challenge him, so we look down as a sign of respect."

Because Korean culture discourages physical contact between strangers, Koreans consider it impolite to touch someone or hand something directly to another. However, Korean shopkeepers did not understand that African Americans, long the target of racial prejudice from whites, felt shunned when their purchases and change were placed on the counter rather than put into their hands. Some African Americans became annoyed because they thought the Koreans simply did not want to touch black people. In many stores, resentment flared on both sides of the counter because neither person knew what the other was really thinking or feeling. This lack of communication was made worse by the language barrier, which kept many Koreans from talking freely with their customers.

The African American community's resentment turned to anger in the spring of 1991, when a 15-year-old black girl named Latasha Harlins was shot and killed by a Korean shopowner after a scuffle over a bottle of juice. As the San Francisco *Chronicle* reported: "For blacks, Harlins was a victim of racial prejudice and a cold-blooded murder over a $1.79 bottle of orange juice. For Korean Americans, her death

was the tragic result of a middle-aged immigrant woman's nerves giving way after weeks of harassment by black gangs." Black rage grew when the shopowner was put on probation instead of being sent to jail.

A little more than a year later, an explosion of rage occurred that changed the face of Los Angeles and forced Americans of all races to ask painful questions about social justice. The violent turmoil began on April 29, 1992, a day that Korean Americans in Los Angeles remember as *Sa-i-gu* (Korean for "four twenty-nine," thus "April twenty-nine"). On that day, a California jury announced its verdict in the trial of four white police officers charged with beating Rodney King, a black man, in the course of arresting him. The jury declared them not guilty, even though the beating had been captured on videotape and seen around the world. When word of the verdict reached the public, the streets of South Central Los Angeles exploded.

The upheaval began when an angry crowd attacked passing motorists and sacked nearby buildings. Despite pleas for calm from city officials and church and community leaders, the violence swept through the South Central district and then spread to other areas. Crowds of mostly blacks and Latinos looted stores and set buildings on fire. Images of fury and destruction appeared on television. The toll in hospital emergency rooms rose, and plumes of smoke thickened over the city. Bus service was canceled, flights were rerouted away from Los Angeles International Airport, and highway exits were closed to keep people from entering the danger zone. The mayor and governor declared a state of emergency and called in 6,000 National Guard troops to try to restore order.

By May 1, the unrest had finally begun to quiet down, and in parts of the stricken area people were beginning to clean up the devastated streets. The devastation was stunning: at least 58 deaths; nearly 2,400 injuries; 7,000 fires; more than 12,000 arrests; $800 million in damages; and 3,100 businesses damaged by fire, vandalism, or looting.

When the violence subsided, many buildings in Koreatown, as well as many Korean businesses in the South Central district, were nothing more than smoldering ruins. More than 2,000 of the businesses that were damaged or destroyed belonged to Koreans. Many of the Koreans felt that they had been specially targeted by black gangs, who incited much of the looting and destruction. "It has been twenty years since Koreans came here," an immigrant woman said sadly. "Everything we worked for is now in flames. It burned in one day." Another said, "We Koreans worked hard to realize our dreams. Now nothing is left but ashes." As they picked through the rubble of their dreams, the dazed Koreans felt both anger and bewilderment.

"I'm totally confused," said a woman who owned a liquor store that was destroyed. "I don't know who I should be angry at." Another store owner said bitterly, "I felt betrayed by the black kids. All my love for them turned to nothing." Many blamed the police for not protecting them. One young man reported that when he called the police to report an attack on his family's store, he was told, "I hope you have insurance, because we can't go down there."

Afterward, people of all races offered many reasons for what had happened. A 66-year-old black woman declared that she was not upset that rioters had burned up the Korean store on her corner. "Now the Koreans run the liquor store and don't let no black people work in there, and they treat black people like they're dogs," she said. "I stopped my grandchildren from going to the little Korean store up on the corner. They was talking to them like they was bad." A black businessman said, "I saw angry people. Furious people. I also saw people who were going to take advantage of the situation. . . . They were hitting Korean businesses. They were looking at people who had abused them in the past."

A Korean American owner of a record store that was looted explained, "I don't think Koreans are entirely blameless. In my opinion, those doing business in the black community don't have the proper understanding to do business there. They can't speak the language or understand black customs. So even if they don't mean to be that way, Korean merchants are perceived as being unfriendly. The way Koreans interact with each other doesn't work in America. On the other hand, the blacks ask us Koreans, 'Why don't you respect us?' But their young kids steal, and the older kids too. How can we respect them?"

A Korean American lawyer felt both "sad and angry" when she witnessed the turmoil in her home city of Los Angeles. "I hear generalizations on both sides of the black-

Korean equation all the time," she said. "It troubles me a lot because black people are not all one way and Korean American people are not all another way. It is very dangerous to make generalizations about people." She added, "What is happening right now is not Korean history, it is American history."

Many Korean Americans agreed that the explosion in Los Angeles should not be regarded as a conflict between African Americans and Korean Americans. They felt that the rage that had been turned against Koreans was an expression

A Korean greengrocer in New York, where Korean Americans have also experienced both success and tragedy.

of the anger and frustration created by black unemployment, poverty, and despair. A store owner said, "Basically, what happened is the fault of the politicans. There's something wrong with the way they're running race relations." It was also the fault of the economy. South Central Los Angeles, like many other inner cities, was filled with boarded-up factories. Businesses had closed or moved away, and there were few jobs for the people left behind.

In the aftermath of the destruction, many Korean Americans in Los Angeles suffered from depression. They felt that their "American dream" had been destroyed. They had always believed that if they worked hard, obeyed the law, and minded their own business, they would succeed. Now their work had gone up in smoke, and they could not understand why. Many of them, unable to afford insurance, were wiped out financially. Even those who had insurance or other resources were not sure whether they wanted to rebuild their businesses. "Financially and emotionally, we're not ready to go back," said a man whose family had lost six small businesses in the inner city. "We are very frustrated and very angry, but also we are afraid." One year after the riot, only 28% of the Korean businesses that were destroyed had been rebuilt.

A Korean community leader and member of the Black-Korean Alliance summed up the feelings of despair felt by many Koreans after the explosion: "People felt so powerless over the last few days. It was a tremendously traumatic experience. It will take some time to heal, and then we have to start the rebuilding process."

But rebuilding must mean more than simply putting up new structures in the place of those that were burned. Soon Chang Kwon, a writer who lives in Los Angeles, has urged his

fellow Korean Americans to "build a bridge to the black community and other communities." One way to build such a bridge, a Korean minister in San Francisco suggested, would be for Korean Americans to become more aware of their roles and responsibilities in the community. Struggling to survive and invest in their futures, he explained, Korean business owners often have no paid employees. They employ only their families, not realizing the resentment this causes in neighborhoods where the unemployment rate, especially among young black men, is very high. Such businesspeople need to find ways to invest in the communities in which they do business, not just in their own families.

This young Korean American will grow up in—and contribute to—an increasingly multicultural, diverse society.

Korean employment of black youth, however, will not produce enough jobs for blacks. Both groups find themselves trapped in cities where manufacturing has declined and where unemployment among African Americans is at an all-time high. Both Korean Americans and African Americans must listen to Rodney King's powerful plea during the days of rage, when he urged people to get along, to work out their differences. But in order to get along, Korean Americans and African Americans will need to rebuild the economies of America's inner cities, and this is a task that demands a national effort.

Chronology

1883–1901 A handful of Korean diplomats, students, workers, and political refugees arrive in Hawaii and the U.S. mainland.

1902 The Korean labor migration begins with the arrival of 20 Korean workers in Hawaii.

1903–5 About 6,700 Koreans emigrate to Hawaii to work on the sugar plantations.

1904 Japan invades Korea.

1905 The Japanese rulers of Korea ban emigration from Korea to Hawaii, greatly reducing the flow of Korean immigrants to Hawaii and the U.S. mainland; the first Korean Christian churches are founded in San Francisco and Los Angeles.

1908 Korean nationalist In-hwan Chang assassinates Durham Stevens in San Francisco.

1910 Japan formally takes control of Korea.

1924 The U.S. Congress passes an immigration law that prevents Asian immigrants from entering the United States.

1941 Japan bombs Pearl Harbor; the United States enters World War II.

1945 At the end of World War II, U.S. and Soviet troops liberate Korea from Japanese domination.

1948 Korea is divided into North Korea and South Korea.

1950–53 The Korean War pits North Korea, backed by the Soviet Union, against South Korea, backed by the United States.

1950–64	Approximately 14,000 Koreans enter the United States as wives or adopted children of American citizens.
1965	The U.S. Congress passes a new immigration act that opens the door for the second wave of Asian immigration.
1970s	Los Angeles' Koreatown begins growing dramatically.
1992	South Central Los Angeles erupts in a racial and class upheaval; more than a thousand Korean businesses are destroyed by fire and looting.

Further Reading

Choy, Bong-Youn. *Koreans in America.* Chicago: Nelson-Hall, 1979.

Hyun, Peter. *Man Sei!: The Making of a Korean American.* Honolulu: University of Hawaii Press, 1986.

Kang, Younghill. *East Goes West.* Chicago: Follett, 1968.

———. *The Grass Roof.* Bound with Mirok Li. *The Yalu Flowers.* New York: Norton, 1975.

Kim, Hyung-chan, and Wayne Patterson. *The Koreans in America: 1882–1974.* Dobbs Ferry, NY: Oceana Publications, 1974.

Kim, Illsoo. *New Urban Immigrants: The Korean Community in New York.* Princeton, NJ: Princeton University Press, 1981.

Kim, Ronyoung. *Clay Walls.* Sag Harbor, NY: Permanent Press, 1986.

Lee, Mary Paik. *Quiet Odyssey: A Pioneer Woman in America.* Edited by Sucheng Chan. Seattle: University of Washington Press, 1990.

Lehrer, Brian. *The Korean Americans.* New York: Chelsea House, 1988.

Light, Ivan, and Edna Bonacich. *Immigrant Entrepreneurs: Koreans in Los Angeles, 1965–1982.* Berkeley and Los Angeles: University of California Press, 1988.

Mayberry, Jodine. *Koreans.* New York: Watts, 1991.

Pai, Margaret K. *The Dreams of Two Yi-Min.* Honolulu: University of Hawaii Press, 1989.

Patterson, Wayne. *The Korean Frontier in America: Immigration to Hawaii, 1896–1910.* Honolulu: University of Hawaii Press, 1988.

Sunoo, Sonia. *Korea Kaleidoscope: Oral Histories.* Davis: University of California, 1982.

Takaki, Ronald. *A Different Mirror: A History of Multicultural America.* Boston: Little, Brown, 1993.

Yu, Diana. *Winds of Change: Korean Women in America.* Silver Spring, MD: Women's Institute Press, 1991.

Yu, Eui-Young, Earl H. Phillips, and Eun Sik Yang, eds. *Koreans in Los Angeles: Prospects and Promises.* Los Angeles: Center for Korean-American and Korean Studies, 1982.

Index

RONALD TAKAKI, the son of immigrant plantation laborers from Japan, graduated from the College of Wooster, Ohio, and earned his Ph.D. in history from the University of California at Berkeley, where he has served both as the chairperson and the graduate advisor of the Ethnic Studies program. Professor Takaki has lectured widely on issues relating to ethnic studies and multiculturalism in the United States, Japan, and the former Soviet Union and has won several important awards for his teaching efforts. He is the author of six books, including the highly acclaimed *Strangers from a Different Shore: A History of Asian Americans,* and the recently published *A Different Mirror: A History of Multicultural America.*

REBECCA STEFOFF is a writer and editor who has published more than 50 nonfiction books for young adults. Many of her books deal with geography and exploration, including the three-volume set *Extraordinary Explorers,* recently published by Oxford University Press. Stefoff also takes an active interest in environmental issues. She served as editorial director for two Chelsea House series—*Peoples and Places of the World* and *Let's Discover Canada.* Stefoff studied English at the University of Pennsylvania, where she taught for three years. She lives in Portland, Oregon.